The Himalayan Cat Owner's Manual.

Facts and information, care, personality, grooming, health and feeding all included.

by

Elliott Lang

Author: Elliott Lang

Published by: IMB Publishing

Table of Contents

Acknowledgements

I have always been in the company of animals. That is the one thing I am most thankful for. My lovely pets have always been around to provide unconditional affection and love when I needed it the most.

My father was instrumental in making me grow fond of animals. He always kept me around animals. I guess he was trying to help me learn how to be tolerant and loving from these amazing creatures. Trust me, some of the biggest life lessons that I have gained have come from these beautiful creatures.

My family, too, has always been hands on with the pets in the household. Whether it was bathing, feeding or taking care of these animals, my family relied on pure instincts and ensured that the animals got the best of everything. These animals were the centre of all our activities. There was not a single day that did not begin with a discussion about these pets. What to feed them? How to take care of a cat or dog that is ailing? What is the most nutritious thing to feed them? These were common dinner table conversations while I was growing up. So, needless to say, I have had a lot of practical training with respect to taking care of different breeds of animals. Sometimes I learnt from my family and sometimes your pet will just tell you what he or she needs. Today, I am in a very privileged place where I can share this information with pet lovers across the globe.

It is my sincere attempt to create a series of books that will help you take care of your pet cats. These books are written with the intent of creating a manual for pet owners. I would have never been able to provide you with so much comprehensive information without the knowledge that I gained from my father, my family and of course my beloved cats.

Foreword

Remember Mr. Jinx, the adorable Himalayan cat from the movie, "Meet the Parents"? Or, how about Colonel Meow, the popular online Himalayan Kitty who held the world record for the longest fur? Well, Himalayan cats have always been media darlings because of their swank and their high glamour quotient. These cats have the beauty of a Persian cat and the grace of a Siamese cat. What more could a cat owner ask for?

This breed was introduced only in the 1930s but has become a rage ever since. Her Highness Queen Victoria owned two blue point Himalayan cats while Martha Stewart owned seven of them! Because of their beauty, these cats are definitely popular with celebrities. However, even people who are not in the limelight have become quite fond of this beautiful breed. Today, it is one of the most preferred breeds in the world. I, too, have been lucky to have owned a lovely Himalayan beauty.

My interactions with my own Himalayan Cat really inspired me to document all the things necessary to give your Himmie a healthy and happy life. I can personally account for several occasions when I had no clue what to do with my cat and how to help him in specific situations.

When I went online or even tried to find books to help me, I realized that the information was so exhaustive that it could intimidate anyone reading it. So, I decided to combine all the frequently asked questions about Himalayan Cats to create a manual for all Himalayan Cat owners.

This book will tell you everything right from where to buy your kittens to how to take care of your cat's health and nutrition. This is perhaps the only book of its kind available exclusively for Himalayan Cat owners.

I really hope you find this book informative and useful. I have invested a great deal of time to research and record the things that I thought Himalayan Cat owners must know. My book is based on personal experiences and interactions. Therefore, I am confident that you will find solutions to any problem that you might have with raising your Himalayan Cat.

Chapter 1: The Himalayan Cat - Introduction

If you have always dreamed of having a cuddly and fuzzy pet, then the Himalayan Cat is the apt breed for you. They are adorably cute as kittens and only grow up to become 'bundles of joy' in every real sense.

The striking blue eyes are not the only appealing quality of this beauty. This cat comes in a variety of colors and has fur that is so soft and warm that you will want to cuddle it all day.

Himalayan cats are extremely loving and gentle and can be easily mistaken to be a Persian cat. Of course, it is a descendant of the Persian cat but it has some unique qualities that make this beauty popular among cat lovers.

The most striking quality of the Himalayan cat is its colored points. Although the most common color for this breed is white or cream, you can find several other colors of points in this cat. It is these colored points that differentiate a Himalayan cat from a Persian Cat. Of course, if you have European friends, they might not be aware of this breed name. In these countries, even the Himalayan cat is known as the Persian cat. Of course, one minute change is that it is referred to as the 'color point Persian' to help them distinguish between the two breeds.

Just to make sure that you do not get confused, here are some features that you can look out for to make sure that you have a Himalayan cat in your home:

The Eyes: Himalayan cats have lovely blue eyes that stand out despite the long fur that grabs all your attention.

Colour: The fur of the cat is usually beige or white all over. However, there are several colors available with the colored points. The most common colors are lilac, seal, chocolate, red, tabby, blue and tortoise.

Fur: The fur is long, no doubt. But what sets the coat of the Himalayan cat apart is the shine of the coat and the inherent thickness of the coat.

The Head: The head of the Himalayan cat varies as per its type. There are basically two breeds of the Himalayan Cat - the doll face and the peke face. The head is rounded in both types but the features are more squished in the peke face in comparison to the doll face.

The Himalayan cat is one of the most popular breeds in the world. Studies show that it is the second most preferred breed of cats globally. Of course, if you look up the list of top ten favorite cats, you may not see the name of the gorgeous Himalayan cat. This is perhaps because the Himalayan cat is not recognized as a separate breed from the Persian. It is listed as a unique breed by the International Cat Fanciers' Association, however.

If you have chosen a Himalayan cat for your home, you are definitely in for a treat. Your Himalayan cat will love to be around you and spend time with you. These cats are quiet and docile, but can make the best companions that you could ever ask for.

a. Types of Himalayan Cats

When we talk about breeds of cats that do not occur naturally, we must be open to different types of breeds. Since these cats are made by crossing two breeds, the permutations and combinations that are possible are many. So, like any other 'man made breed' of cats, even the Himalayan cat comes in two basic types, the extreme and the traditional breed.

Extreme Himalayan v/s Traditional Himalayan

The extreme and the traditional Himalayan cats are also known as the original and the doll-face Himalayan cat respectively. Most often, the extreme Himalayan cat is seen in pet shows while the traditional Himalayan cat is the breed that people prefer to bring home.

The common feature between the two breeds is that they have the typical wide eyes, the large and chubby cheeks, small ears, round and large head and the prominent chin. With the traditional Himalayan, the biggest difference that you will notice is the placement of the nose. The nose is set much lower on the face and has a very light break. The nose is snub and pink, giving it the 'doll face' appearance.

The face itself is not flat in the traditional Himalayan cat. The best feature of this cat is the lip that curves upwards. Because of this, the cat appears very sweet and almost looks like it is constantly smiling. It is because of this feature that the traditional Himalayan cat is fancied by several cat lovers.

With the extreme Himalayan cat, you will notice that the face is severely flattened. Because of this, there are several medical problems that the extreme Himalayan cat faces. He might have difficulty in breathing and is most likely to have skin infections due to excessive tearing. The Traditional Cat's Association always promotes traditional breeds because they are healthier and are a lot more comfortable to take care of.

However, if you intend to display your kitty at shows, the extreme type will suit you best. Either way, be prepared for some serious kitty love.

b. Persian or Himalayan? The Million Dollar Question

It is quite common for breeders to cheat unsuspecting cat lovers when it comes to buying a Himalayan Cat. Since the Himalayan Cat and the Persian cat are so similar in their appearance, it is quite possible for you to bring home the wrong breed. Especially when they are kittens, the Himalayan Cat and the Persian Cat are identical to look at. The Himalayan kittens have no color points until they are about 3-4 months old. So are there any significant differences that you must look out for? Why, certainly! Here are a few obvious characteristics that will help you make the right choice of breed for your home.

History of the Breeds

We will talk about the History of the Himalayan Cat in a lot more detail in the coming chapters. However, knowing the history of the breed will help you ask your breeder the right questions to make sure that you are indeed getting a Himalayan Cat and not a Persian Cat.

The Persian cat was discovered by an Italian traveler named Peitro della Valle. He found this breed of silky haired cat in Persia. They were originally grey in color and had a much longer face than the Persian cat that we see today. The cute, pleasant faced breed that we see today is the result of crossing the original Persian cat with another breed called the Turkish Angora. With this crossing came several other colors of the Persian cat.

On the other hand, the Himalayan Cat is a recently created breed of cats. They were produced by crossing the Persian cat with a Siamese cat to produce the typical colored points that we see in the beautiful Himalayan Cat.

Color

This is the most significant difference between the Himalayan cat and the Persian Cat. The most important thing for cat buyers and cat lovers to note is that whatever color you find a Himalayan cat in, be sure that you will not find a Persian cat in the same color. So, this means, you will never find a Persian cat that is tabby, lilac, tortoise shell and dual colored.

The eye color must also be paid attention to when you are purchasing a Himalayan cat. If the eye color is anything else but blue, chances are that you actually have a Persian cat. While the Himalayan cat will only have blue eyes, the Persian cat can have a variety of eye colors including green and bright yellow.

As for the color of the fur, the Himalayan cat will most often have colored points. These colors are similar to the Siamese cat. They usually come in shades of blue, tabby or brown. They are also named according to the colored points. A Himalayan cat is known as a "flame point" if the color of the point is red or tabby. On the other hand, it is known as a "lynx point" when it has brown color points. In the female Himalayan cat, one can find several color points like orange, black and even tortoiseshell colors. This color point feature is never observed in a Persian cat.

The Voice

Persian cats are almost always silent. They are not as vocal as normal domesticated cats. Of course, there are always exceptions. On the other hand, the Himalayan cat is extremely vocal and has a very harsh voice. Their voice is also very strong, much like the Siamese cat. In comparison to the Siamese cat, however, the Himalayan cat is much quieter.

Usually, both Persian cats and the Himalayan cats are good around human company. Still, they are never too keen to voice their needs. It is up to their owners to figure out and fulfil their needs. These breeds are extremely aristocratic in their behavior. So, you might want to be prepared to have a new master in the house when you bring them in.

Why do people get confused between these two breeds?

Well, like we mentioned before, the Persian cat and the Himalayan cat are strikingly similar in their appearance. To begin with, they both have the same silky, long fur. Grooming and taking care of both the breeds is almost the same. In addition to this, they have the trademark flat face or doll-faced head, which often confuses cat lovers.

The temperament of both the cats is almost the same. They have the same health problems and will require the same kind of medical attention. As a result, when someone describes their

Persian cat or their Himalayan cat to you, they may seem almost identical.

Just to make sure you get the right breed, you must ask your breeder about the parents of the kitten. That is a sure shot way of knowing what breed you are actually purchasing.

c. General Information about the Himalayan Cat

Weight in the Male- > 12 lbs/ 5 kgs

Weight in the Female- 7-12 lbs/3-5 kgs

Eye Color- Deep Blue

Life Span- 9-15 years

Attention Demand- Moderate

Shedding of Fur- High

Length of Fur- Long

Texture of Coat – Fine, long and thick

Color- Blue Point, Lilac Point, Seal Point, Red Point, cream Point

Allergenic Property – High

Grooming Need - High

Associations that recognize the breed - CFA. ACA, TICA

Prevalence of the Breed- Second most owned breed in the world

Chapter 2: History of the Himalayan Cat

From the name of this breed, one would expect its origins to be somewhere around the Himalayan area. This seems quite right considering its long and thick fur that is apt for a cat that needs to brave the cold weather in the Himalayan area.

However, the truth is that the Himalayan cat was first bred in the United States. Then why is it not called the American cat? Well, the reason is that the name of the cat has nothing to do with the place of origin. This breed is actually named after the Himalayan rabbit which has color points similar to the Himalayan cat. Well, cat breeders sure do put in a lot of thought into naming the beautiful cat breeds that they create.

The Himalayan cat was first created in the 1930's by Virgina Cobb and Dr. Clyde Keeler. The primary objective of this breeding program was to understand the methods to create a color-point cat with long hair. After five years of experimentation and trials, their breakthrough came in the year 1937 when they first created a Himalayan kitten. This cat was named 'Newton's Debutante'. They also published an article in the American Journal of heredity where the details of the experiment involved in the creation of the Himalayan cat were recorded. Once they had achieved the desired results, this program was abandoned.

The origin of this breed in England is a rather interesting story. When a stray cat named 'Bubastis Georgina" made her way into the Briarry Cattery, she inspired the creation of a new breed in that country. You see, this was no ordinary cat, it was a long haired color point. So, the breeder in this cattery, Brian Stirling Webb started a new program with Mrs. S M Harding to develop more such cats in England.

During the 1950s, the breeding of the Himalayan Cat received new momentum. A lady named Marguerita Goforth was highly inspired by a cat that belonged to her friend. While she was taking care of this long haired color point cat for her friend, Marguerita, who was also a breeder, decided that she must start a breeding program to create more such cats.

Her friend's cat, named "Princess Himalayan Hope" was actually adopted from the San Diego Humane Society. After seeking permission from the owners of the cat, she set out to create the ideal pet cat- a Persian cat with the coloring of the Siamese cat.

Characteristics of the Persian Cat and the Siamese Cat

In order to understand the history of this breed, it is important to know the characteristics of the breeds that were used to create it. Then, you will be able to point out all traits have been passed on to the visual treat called the Himalayan Cat.

The Persian Cat

The Cat Fanciers' Association lists the Persian cat as one of the most popular pure bred cats in the world. Needless to say, the breed standards are also extremely high. Persian cats are known for their visual appeal and are considered great home cats because of their docile nature.

This breed was discovered in the Middle East by an Italian traveler. When it was introduced in Europe, cat lovers fell in love with this adorable looking breed. During the 19th Century, the Persian cat had become so popular that Queen Victoria herself had two Persian cats in her palace.

The most stunning quality of this cat is its fur. The long, thick and silky coat of this breed is a delight to any cat lover. Just like the Himalayan cat, the Persian cat too has a sweet expression and comes in two varieties - the doll face and the flat face. The typical pink nose and the rounded, small ears are qualities that the Himalayan cat has inherited from the Persian Cat.

The important personality trait of the Persian cat is that it will only pick one favourite member in the family. He will demand attention from this family member and will insist on curling on the lap of this person. Persian cats are not very vocal and are seldom attached to other members of the family.

The Siamese Cat

The color point fur of the Siamese cat is its most striking quality. Color point means that certain areas of the fur like the face, the tail, the tips of the paws and the ears will have a darker shade in comparison to the rest of the cat's body. The colorpoint feature of the Siamese cat was of primary concern to the breeders of the Himalayan cat. They were quite clear that they wanted a cat with fur like the Persian cat and coloring like the Siamese cat.

Besides the physical traits, the Himalayan cat also has certain personality traits that are similar to the Siamese cat. The Himalayan cat is vocal and has a voice that is quite similar to the Siamese cat. The elegance of the Siamese cat is a quality that you simple cannot miss in the Himalayan Cat. The Siamese cat is also quite attached to its family and will most often not survive if left on its own or abandoned.

The beauty of the Himalayan cat is that it has the right personality traits of each breed. This makes it the ideal pet to have. It is no wonder that cat lovers have chosen the Himalayan cat to be part of their household more than any other breed of cats. Not only are these beauties the perfect eye candy, they are also the most adorable companions to have.

Chapter 3: Personality of the Himalayan Cat

The choice of cats made to breed the Himalayan cat was rather strange. These two cats were poles apart in terms of their appearance and their personality. While one was short haired, the other was long haired. While one was a complete attention seeker, the other was quite aloof. So, the resulting breed was the ideal one for everyone. A perfect blend of all the desirable qualities in these breeds gave us the Himalayan cat, or as we would fondly call it, "The Himmie".

The Perfect Balance

The beauty of the Himalayan cat lies in the fact that it is a perfect balance between the Persian cat and the Siamese cat. Several blogs that have reviews by Himalayan cat owners who previously owned a Persian cat or a Siamese cat show this common thread. They seem to have inherited the right qualities in the right amount, making them extremely sought after.

The first thing that you will be glad that the Himalayan cat inherited from its Persian parent is the temperament. The Himalayan cat is just as docile and gentle as the Persian cat. They love to be petted and they will also be very gentle and loving in return. However, unlike the Persian cat, the Himalayan cat does not come across as an aloof, one master pet. That is the balance that this breed maintains. The Himalayan cat will get along quite well with almost all members of your family, including your other pets and even little children.

The Siamese traits that you will be thankful for is the voice and the playfulness. The Himalayan cat is not as vocal as the Siamese cat but it is definitely a lot more vocal than the Persian cat. The voice is also gentle and soothing. But, you can be sure that he will not be as talkative as the Siamese cat. So, if you had a Siamese cat whose constant mewing was a bother, you should opt for the Himalayan cat that is talkative, but in the right amount.

When you are bored, your Himmie will make a great companion. They are extremely playful and will spend time with you when you need it. This is another quality that is inherited in the right amount. While Persian cats are simply too laid back, the Siamese cat will demand a lot of attention. The Himalayan cat is not as demanding as the Siamese cat but maintains a very neutral and rather pleasant 'cattitude' unlike the royal Persian cat.

Himalayan cats are great pets to have. You will be glad that you chose this breed as it will keep you company when you need it and will also let you relax when you are too tired or exhausted to play. One thing that is adorable about the Himalayan cat is that they know exactly how you feel and will respond perfectly to that, making you feel a lot more at home.

Laid Back

Himalayan cats love to chill. They will never be too excited to handle or even too destructive like some of the more playful breeds. They will be very happy perched on the refrigerator or in just some warm corner of the house. The good thing about the Himalayan cat is that they love attention. But do not crave it. If you need to leave the cat alone in the day, he will be happy to laze around in his favorite corner of the house. On the other hand, if he feels too neglected or unloved, he will talk it out with his evidently displeased mews and will also covey his sadness through his great big blue eyes.

No matter how many safe hideouts you make for your Himalayan cat, his ideal resting space will be your lap. If your pet finds a vacant space on your lap, be sure that he will leap right up and make himself comfortable. Himalayan Cats are not affectionate with just one particular person like their Persian ancestors. They will be just as cuddly with any other member of your family. But, beware of strangers interacting with the Himmie. While some good natured fellows will get along well with strangers, most

Himalayan cats are awkward around unknown people and can threaten strangers with their sharp claws.

The Himmie is particularly fond of human company. They will seldom leave your company and will always be right beside you. If not on your lap, your Himmie will be curled up around your feet or will gently rub itself against your legs to make sure that you are not going anywhere.

They also have very accurate biological clocks and will make it a point to wake you up each morning at the same exact time. Perhaps these intelligent beauties can tell time. Either way, your Himalayan cat will bring discipline in your life.

The Himmie also loves to participate in all your household chores with you. If you are vacuuming your carpet, you can enjoy the sight of your Himmie wrestling with the vacuum cleaner. If you are folding your laundry, your Himmie will be perched at the exact same spot where you are most likely to put away your clothes. Of course, he/she will end up wrestling with the folded clothes, making a mess for you to clean again.

One adorable quality of the Himalayan cat is that they will follow you around your house until you sit down and let him curl up on your lap. They also love rubbing themselves against you, leaving large amounts of fur on your clothes!

The Himalayan cat will make sure that you have no reason to complain. The amount of love that these cats have to give is exceptional. They will, most definitely, share your bed. They will curl up beside your feet or neck and may even make you their mattress when they are in the mood. When you have a Himmie, make sure you understand that you and your cat are inseparable. Even if you don't think so, the Himmie will ensure that you do.

Pecking Order

If you are considering bringing a pet home, the most important factor to consider is the other members of your family, who will compete for your love and attention. Yes, this is where you think about the children and the other pets in your home. Whenever you make a new addition to the family, you must rest assured that no one will be harmed or no one will be emotionally distressed. With the Himalayan cat, this is usually not an issue. This breed is extremely gentle and has great adaptability.

When it comes to children, the Himalayan cat is extremely tolerant towards them. They will particularly enjoy the company of older children. If you have children under the age of six, never leave them unsupervised with the Himalayan cat. Of course, they are not a threat to the child, but the child can be extremely threatening to your Himalayan cat. If the cat feels uncomfortable or is frightened by a sudden push or touch from the child, he is less likely to attack. He will simply slither away and hide in a secure place in the house. But, he will not like it if your child coaxes him to get out of the hide out. That is when he/she will get a little defensive.

The Himalayan cat is not the most dog friendly cat. At the same time, he/she will not attack or dislike the dog. However, he may like to maintain a safe distance from a dog who obviously seems like a huge and playful threat to your medium sized Himalayan cat. The breed of the dog that you have at home is extremely important. If the breed is overtly active and playful, you can expect your Himalayan cat to give him the cold shoulder. Not because he feels threatened, but simply because a Himalayan cat hates being forced to play or run around. With a playful dog that might chase the cat around, don’t expect a very happy Himalayan cat.

Himalayan cats are extremely sweet and will never be bad company for other cats in your house. They will simply not get too friendly or affectionate with other cats. In case you have a male Himalayan cat, remember that he is the quintessential alpha male. He will be dominating over the other cats in your household. With ample training and the right introduction, you will not see any cat fights in your home.

The Himalayan cat often is too docile to protect itself. He will choose flight over fight any day. So, if you have pets or children in your home, make sure that you have several easy hiding spaces in your home. They must be safe for the cat and must be inaccessible by the pet or child that he is running away from.

Usually, the pecking order with Himalayan cats is as follows:

- Children

- Dogs

- Other cats

Of course, this preference changes from one cat to another, You cannot expect every Himalayan cat to have the same pecking order. However, you can make sure that things do not turn ugly in your household. The only thing that a Himalayan cat dislikes is being manhandled. If any touch is painful for the cat, he will avoid that touch forever. So, if you have children at home, remind them to leave your precious kitty alone once in a while.

As for the other pets, try to avoid unsupervised interactions. Usually, a Himalayan cat will ensure that he stays away from unpleasant situations. However, to be on the safer side, you might want to watch over your cats and dogs when they are together. Of course, if the animals get along well, you will see that they can become friends for life. If you need proof, you can treat yourself to thousands of adorable home videos online of Himalayan cats and other pets in the house. It is endearing to see how these completely different breeds and species can live under the same roof in peace and complete harmony.

Intelligence

Himalayan Cats are easily the most deceptive cats. They will pretend to be extremely sluggish and rather dull when they want their 'me' time. Au contraire, the Himalayan cat is highly intelligent. The proof of this fact lies in the fact that you can actually train the Himalayan cat to fit perfectly into your household. They do not take too much time to acquire new skills and are rather smart despite the popular belief that they are dumb cats.

With the Himalayan cat, you need to constantly stimulate its brain. You can keep him mentally active by giving him several puzzles and toys.

Himalayan cats love to learn new tricks. You can, with some patience, train your kitty to listen to voice commands just like a dog. They are quick learners and will respond to new lessons quite positively. They are not as lazy as they are perceived to be and can actually be very good playmates.

Curiosity is a quality that the Himalayan cat displays moderately. You will rarely see your cat prodding at objects or poking around your home. However, they will be highly curious about you. They want to know what is up with you, always. You will notice your kitty walking around you with, ever so inquisitively, enquiring about your day by simply staring at you. They will also sit on high shelves and simply watch over the household. They are also curious enough to learn things.

Another quality that you will notice in the Himalayan cat is that they will acquire skills like opening the door and even getting their toys out when they want. Himalayan cats are not satisfied with one toy. They need several toys to stimulate their minds. In case a Himalayan cat is not given the kind of attention or the right amount of mental stimulation, they run the risk of becoming extremely lazy and even aloof.

So, even if your friends or some poorly informed blog writers claim that the Himalayan cat is a dumb cat, make sure you consider it just as intelligent as any other cat breed that exists.

Activity Level

The Himalayan cat is so laid back that people often consider it a lazy cat. The complete truth is that the Himalayan cat is not so much lazy as he is moody. When he wants to, the Himalayan cat will go all out to entertain you and play with you.

Remember that the Himalayan cat is a descendent of the Siamese cat who is the ideal 'dog-cat'. Needless to say, the Himmie too has certain qualities that will remind you of the Siamese cat. They love to play fetch and will also heed to commands and calls. Himalayan cats can be quite the acrobats when they are in a playful mood. They will jump from shelves to counters and might even wrestle curtains when they are up to it.

Of course, there is no chance that you can leash train the Himalayan cat. However, if you want a dog without the responsibility of walking it, you will love the Himalayan cat. They will be the most loving, playful companions. They love to run in circles around you and also love to follow you around the house.

They definitely love to be in your company. However, remember this: your Himalayan cat is the master of his will. If he is not in the mood, he will never come out of his hiding and play with you. Sometimes, he might just want to sit around and punch a ball of wool around. If he is in this lazy mood, don't force him to play with you. He will not appreciate it and will stay away from you for a good amount of time.

Watching your Himalayan cat is extremely entertaining. While the Himalayan cat demands several toys, he will have one particular toy that he will hold on to all day. He will play with this toy, he will take it around the house, punch that toy and even drown it in buckets and tubs of water. It is really entertaining to watch your Himmie treat this toy like a real person or like a living being. Also, the way they are so inquisitive about something as simple as a spool of thread will make you want to just gobble of this bundle of cuteness!

The Himmie is considered the most talkative of all cat breeds. These cats love to tell their owners about their day by purring whenever they are around them. They will talk back when spoken to. If you like talking to your Himmie, he will definitely respond with soft purrs and meows.With a Himalayan Cat, you will find yourself a true companion. They are very patient creatures who are extremely attached to their owners. They like to be cared for and loved. The most amazing thing about the Himmie is that it is a highly understanding cat that is sensitive enough to react to your moods perfectly. If you are happy, your Himmie will rejoice with you. If you are upset, your Himmie will curl up close to you and will never leave your side. Overall, this is one of the most compassionate cat breeds that you can ask for.

Summary of the Himalayan Cat Personality

To help you understand better, here is a simple chart that will rate your Himalayan Cat's personality traits out of 5. These are ratings based on the response of several Himalayan Cat owners. This chart will make it easier for you to decide between the Himmie and other cat breeds.

- Affection towards Owner- 5/5
- Adaptability- 4/5
- Playfulness- 3/5
- Compatibility with Other Cats- 3/5
- Compatibility with Dogs- 3/5
- Compatibility with Children- 3/5
- Intelligence- 4/5
- Activity Level- 3/5

Chapter 4: Indoor Cat or Outdoor Cat?

If you are living in an apartment, having a pet can pose a slight dilemma. Very few apartments provide your pet with ample space to play around and exercise. So, people opt out of owning a pet as they feel guilty for confining them to the small space inside the apartment. If you love to have pets at home but just avoid it because you live in an apartment, the Himalayan Cat is the most ideal pet for you.

Himalayan Cats are indoor cats by choice. It actually loves being indoors, cuddled up in the warmest corners of your home. Unlike most cats, the Himalayan is not an independent cat. It does not like being left in the open for too long. Even if you do take your Himmie out occasionally, you must make sure that you are around it all the time as these cats tend feel a sense of despair when they are alone.

Of course, the Himalayan cat will enjoy being left to himself during the day. They are usually very comfortable in their homes. As a matter of fact, it is safer to have long haired cats at home. When they are out, they might contract skin diseases and also parasitic infections.

There are several reasons why people think that keeping a cat indoors is unfair. Some of the most common myths associated with keeping a cat indoors are:

Lack of exercise can lead to weight issues

It is not mandatory for a cat to go outdoors to get the exercise that it requires. Especially with a breed like the Himmie, it is very easy to prompt them to stay active, even indoors. All you need to do is place a cat tree that he can climb. Cats also love to sharpen their claws on these cat trees. Himalayan Cats are naturally playful. This means that you can give him toy mice and other pet toys to play with. Even a ball of thread or a paper box can become a great playing tool for your pet. The most important thing with an indoor cat is the environment that it lives in. If you can make your home comfortable for the cat to run around and play in, you need not worry about taking him outdoors for some exercise.

It is not possible to domesticate a cat to stay indoors

This is not true, especially with the Himalayan Cat. This breed opts to stay indoors. As for the sunshine and natural environment required by them, they will just enjoy these sights and sounds from a window sill. One of the most important Himalayan Cat characteristics is that they will voluntarily stay close to you and walk with you when you take them outdoors. So, you don't even have to worry about getting the cat the amount of outdoor time that it requires. Most cat breeders might recommend an enclosure to keep your cat safe outdoors. However, with a Himmie there is absolutely no need to use any cage or enclosure.

The pet might urinate and dirty the house

Cats as a species are very easy to toilet train. All you need to do is teach them to use the litter box. With an intelligent cat like the Himmie, there is no need to worry about getting the cat toilet trained. One thing that most cat owners observe is that after sometime, the cat urinates outside the box. This is only an indication that the litter box is too dirty. It is the cat's way of telling its owner that it is time to have the litter box cleaned up. Most owners think that this behavior is an indication that the cat needs to go outside. Sometimes, it could be an indication that your cat may have some medical requirements. If your cat continues to litter outside the box even after you have cleaned it, make sure you consult a veterinarian.

The cat might scratch and ruin the furniture

It is true that cats love to keep their claws sharp. So, it is natural for them to scratch hard surfaces as a mechanism to trim and sharpen their claws. If your cat is not trained, then you can expect your furniture to be ruined in just a few days. The solution to this does not come from trimming the nails of your cat. The behavior will persist. The best thing to do would be to provide your cat with a cat tree. In case your cat continues to damage other surfaces in spite of providing him with a tree, you must observe the types of surfaces that he likes to sharpen his nails on. All you need to do is cover the cat tree with that material. Each cat has its own preference when it comes to the material that it chooses to scratch. In order to train your cat to use only the cat tree, you may also spray scents like catnip in order to attract the cat to the tree.

It is unhygienic to have a cat at home

Cats usually tend to walk on high surfaces like kitchen cabinets and shelves. In case you do not find this comfortable or hygienic, you can train the cat to only occupy certain high spaces. For instance, clear a corner on your highest shelf and spray some catnip to attract the cat. It is also possible to train your cat to stay away from the kitchen. In any case, cats are extremely clean creatures. They are constantly bathing or cleaning themselves. Another thing with an indoor cat like the Himmie; the amount of contaminants that it brings in is a lot lesser than an outdoor cat.

Pregnant Women get infected by cats

One very common reason for most people to keep cats outdoors is the presence of a pregnant woman in the household. Many believe that women who are pregnant can contract a disease called Toxoplasmosis if they come into contact with cat feces by accident. Unknown to many, this disease is most often caused by the consumption of uncooked meat. However, in order to be safe, pregnant women should always wear gloves while cleaning litter boxes. The cat is not a threat to the wellbeing of the pregnant woman and can be allowed to stay indoors without the danger of any infection.

Now that we have busted the myths about indoor cats, you might also want to consider some rather logical reasons to keep your cat indoors. When you have a cat like the Himmie that loves to stay indoors, you will never have to really worry about the wellbeing of your cat.

Why is it better to have an indoor cat?

There are several reasons why an indoor cat like the Himmie is a more convenient option. Here are a few things that you might want to consider if you are thinking of choosing an outdoor cat over an indoor cat.

- Traffic is one of the biggest reasons to keep a cat indoors. If you live close to a highway or reside on a street that is relatively busy, you might want to consider a Himmie that will spend most of its time indoors. Even the smallest accident can be fatal for your cat or might result in serious injuries.

- Cats that roam outdoors are most susceptible to infections from other cats. Feline Immunodeficiency Virus or Feline Leukemia is quite common in cats that roam outside. These diseases are usually transmitted from one cat to another. Both the diseases mentioned above are fatal for cats. If you allow your cat to roam freely, there are also several possibilities of cat fights with other stray cats in the neighborhood. This leads to injuries and abscesses that make it hard for both the owner and the cat. Not only do these injuries cause a lot of pain to your pet, they will also cost you several hundreds of dollars to take care of and treat. If your cat has not been properly vaccinated, then it runs the risk of several other diseases that are prevalent in the outdoors.

- Parasites are common issues faced by cats. It is very easy for fleas to attack your cat if it is usually strolling freely in the outdoors. Some fleas may also carry diseases that are deadly for the cat as well as its owners. Some ticks also have the potential to paralyze the cat permanently or even kill it if not treated correctly. Your cat can also be infected by fungi like ringworm. Ringworm can be passed on from the cat to its owner quite easily. Although it is not a deadly disease, ringworm usually recurs in cats and is not easy to treat or get rid of. With a long-haired breed like the

Himalayan cat, tackling these parasites and germs is particularly difficult.

- If your cat is outdoors often, there are several other dangers that it will encounter. Domesticated cats are usually not able to defend themselves against animals like dogs, opossums and snakes and will either end up being seriously injured or even die due to these attacks. If your cat ventures into wrong territories by mistake, it becomes vulnerable to these attacks. Cats are also susceptible to attacks from people as well.

- A cat that is allowed to roam outdoors is most likely to get lost. They may be stolen to be used in labs. In many horrifying instances, cats are killed for trade of fur and even extremist religious practices. So it is best that you either opt for a cat that stays indoors or at least ensure that it has a collar with information to identify it. According to statistics, close to 10% of cats rescued in animal shelters are not reclaimed by their owners.

- Skin cancer is a problem with most cats. In case of cats with dark fur, the threat of skin cancer due to excessive exposure to the sun is more prevalent. While it may not be such a big concern for a cat that has thick, protective fur like the Himalayan cat, you can never be too sure. If you live in a country or a part of the world where skin cancer is highly prevalent, you must consider protecting your cat from exposure to sunlight. Many cat owners neglect the importance of keeping a cat in an enclosure when left outdoors. You must ensure that the enclosure has enough places for the cat in the shade and stay away from the sun.

- You might also face several social problems when you allow your cat to roam outside. It is possible that your cat litters your neighbor's garden or simply ruins a beautiful flower bed. In either case, you might find yourself quarrelling endlessly with your neighbor. It is impossible to locate and control a cat that is used to the outdoors.

- Although there are several myths surrounding the need for cats to be aloof and independent in the outdoors, you can prove them all wrong with your Himalayan Cat. The fact that the cat loves to stay with its owners shows that it is made to be indoors. If you feel like your cat is getting bored of the indoors, all you have to do is put in a bit of effort to make the environment more interesting. Especially with a highly intelligent cat like the Himmie, you must try to include puzzle toys and other stimulating activities in its routine. You must make sure you spend time with your Himmie to keep him healthy and happy.

Contrary to traditional beliefs, a cat that stays indoors is known to be healthier and happier. Considering all the threats that you are protecting it from, there is no reason why you should not believe this. Research proves that cats that are allowed to stay indoors also have a longer life than cats that are allowed to roam freely.

However, there are some cat owners who are not particularly fond of keeping the cat indoors. Himalayan Cat owners however must be willing to keep them in the house. If you are insistent on having a Himalayan Cat but are uncertain about keeping it indoors, you must ensure that you provide it with a good enclosure.

This is the only way to ensure that your cat gets the benefits of staying outdoors while being protected from the dangers that are prevalent. We will discuss in detail about cat enclosures in the following chapters.

Chapter 5: Bringing a Cat Home

With a cat like the Himmie, introduction to new people and new surroundings is not at all a challenge. Since these cats are friendly and adaptive by nature, you will find it a lot easier to prepare the cat for your family and prepare your family for the new entrant.

Pets are wonderful. However, it takes a little bit of effort from your end to make sure that your Himmie feels safe and stays safe in the new environment that he/she is being introduced to. Here are some tips on how you can prepare your home and your family for a cat:

Getting your home ready for a pet

There are several items in the house that might jeopardize the safety of your cat. The Himalayan Cat, especially, is very curious by nature. Because of this trait, they may get injured if the house is not prepared well. If you are bringing home a Himmie kitten, especially, you must prepare the house well. You must make sure that the following things are away from the new cat.

Plants and pots: If you have indoor plants, you must make sure that they are not easily accessible. Some of these plants can even be toxic for the cat. Plants like rhododendron, azalea, ivy and poinsettia are especially dangerous for cats. Cats usually crave greenery and might play with or prod these plants, ending up with serious consequences.

Wires and strings: Cats love to play with loose strings. They will just follow these strings or even chew the ends. If it is an electric wire, it becomes hazardous not only for the cat but for the owners as well. On the other hand, strings and rubber bands may be swallowed by your cat, making it choke or even suffer internal injuries from entangled strings in the intestines.

Doors and Windows: Make sure all the doors and windows in your home are closed. When a cat is placed in an unfamiliar setting, there are chances that it will try to get out. Even though the Himmie is an indoor cat by nature, it may feel threatened in a new atmosphere. All the doors and windows must be secured in such a way that it cannot be opened by a cat.

Other items: You must make sure that all toxic items are not available easily to the cat. If you have cans with pesticides or insecticides, make sure that you keep them in locked cabinets. Even cleaning material like sprays and fluids are extremely dangerous if left around. Any item that might be potentially hazardous to the cat will have a label to indicate it. Therefore, whenever you bring any chemical into your household, keep it away from its reach.

It is also the responsibility of the cat owner to ensure that they use some common sense while preparing the house for the cat. Look around and remove all the items that you think may harm the cat. Breakable items, chemicals and easily swallowable items are dangerous for the cat. If there are any areas in the house where the cat may get stuck or can squeeze into, make sure you have it closed properly.

Preparing your family for a pet

Everyone living in the house must be prepared for the arrival of the cat. Whoever you are sharing your house with must be informed about the changes that might be made to accommodate the cat in your home. They must be prepared to be patient with the cat in order to give it ample time to adjust to the new surroundings that it is in. Only when your new pet is comfortable in the house will everyone be allowed to handle it and play with it. With a cat that is as friendly as the Himmie, you will be surprised at how easy this phase is.

It is also important to ensure that every member in the family has a check list of Do's and Don'ts with respect to the new pet. You must establish rules like keeping doors and windows closed, keeping chemicals locked away and also putting food away to make sure that the cat is safe. One very important instruction is to check washers and dryers before turning them on.

Give your cat a Bonding Room

From the day that your cat has arrived in your home, do not expect it to wander all over the house. It is natural for the cat to pick one spot in the house and stay there until it is well acquainted with the surroundings. Cats will also hide for a few days. This is only natural as he/she may not be very comfortable with the change in environment.

It is a good idea to choose this room for him. When you bring your pet home, set him down in a dedicated room called the 'Bonding Room'. Do not disturb the cat. Just shut the door on your way out and let the cat be. This is a very important step because you will be giving your cat a 'territory' to gain control over. Leaving him alone will make sure that he is not too anxious to explore the new area.

You can make your pet feel more welcome in the room by placing some water and food in the room. You might have to leave a litter tray in the room as well. But make sure you keep the litter tray as far away from the food tray as possible. By nature, cats are extremely clean creatures and will not appreciate eating close to the litter tray. If you want the room to be more comforting for your kitty, you can even get special cat perfumes like the "*Feliway diffuser*" to keep the cat calm and happy. With these special perfumes, your cat will be able to relax even in a completely strange setting. They are all available at popular pet stores and even with your vet.

It is important to keep some bedding for the cat. Once the cat gets accustomed to a soft cushion, blanket or a cat bed, it will never sleep elsewhere. To attract a cat to this sleeping place, you can leave some catnip toys or other toys. A cat like the Himmie will most often prefer to collect items that it loves to play with and bring it to the bedding area. Allow him to do this as he will feel more comfortable with things of his own preference.

Leave the carrier in the bonding room. You can even look for cat tunnels and place them in the room. Creating a space for a new cat to hide in is a great idea. Of course, the cat will only hide in places that he feels really safe in. You cannot control that but it is good to leave him enough options.

What should you be prepared for?

Although there are several blogs that will tell you that the Himmie is extremely comfortable in the presence of human beings, the time that the cat takes to adjust to a new place varies. There are several habits and behavior patterns that your cat may display. There is no need to be alarmed or even disappointed with them. All you need to make sure of is that you are prepared to give your new pet time to get used to you. The most common observation with cats is the time that they take to get out of their bonding room.

Some cats stay confined to this bonding room for several days. It does not mean that your cat dislikes you. Once your cat feels secure, it will be out. Unlike dogs, there is no way you can persuade your cat to come out of hiding.

There are several things that the cat needs to get accustomed to before he decides to venture out into other spaces in the house. The smells and sounds around him are the first things that he must get accustomed to. There are several sounds that are new for him. Your voice, the sound of the telephone, the sound of your car starting in the driveway and all other sounds that seem quite ordinary to us are a big deal for your Himmie.

There are several smells like the smell of your furniture and carpeting that he/she must become familiar with. Of course there is your smell to get used to too. It is through these pieces of information that the cat analyses how safe the environment is from him.

To make sure that you also allow him to get used to the house, try to avoid the following:

- Loudspeakers while watching movies

- Vacuuming the bonding room

- Hosting loud and noisy parties

- Inviting all your friends and family to see your new pet

- Constantly trying to pick up the cat and pet it

When your cat is ready, he/she will come to you without you even trying. Especially with the Himmie, you can be certain that he/she will crave your touch and warmth. Ideally, it takes between 3- 7 days for a cat to get accustomed to the space. However, there are simple things that you can do to make the bonding experience easier for your beautiful Himmie.

Chapter 6: Bonding With the Himmie

You can begin simple activities within a few hours of bringing your cat to your home. Of course, the idea is not to overwhelm the cat but to allow it to start noticing your presence and accepting it.

The First Few Hours

You must never reach for the cat or try to cuddle in the beginning. If your cat is not nervous by nature, he may just come to you on his own. What you should do, however, is visit the cat regularly. Walk into the bonding room, sit on the floor or a low seated chair for a while and call out to him in a voice that is soothing. It is okay for you to walk in and out of the house as long as you leave him alone for a couple of hours in between. Even if it takes several sessions to get your cat to even greet you, don't lose your patience.

In case there are children in your family, make sure that they visit the cat only when they are accompanied by an adult. At least in the initial days, this is mandatory. The reason to take this precaution is that children might get excited at the sight of the cat. If they startle the cat, he might just become anxious and even scratch or harm the child. So, never let children near the cat without proper supervision.

Make time for your cat

The Himmie loves attention. If you do not give your Himmie the time he requires, it is quite likely for him to end up feeling depressed. Make enough time to spend with your cat. You do not have to play with him necessarily. Just make your presence felt in the room. If there are several people living in your house, take turns to visit the cat. Just hang around in the room and allow the cat to get used to you.

Playtime

You will know that your cat is getting used to the bonding room by his behavior. He will not continue to hide from you. With Himalayan Cats, you will know that they are ready for you as they will want to leave their scent on your. They will affectionately rub themselves against your legs. However, if you try to touch them, they may resist it in the beginning. To lure your cat towards you, you can make use of toys. There is no better toy than a shoelace or a piece of string. All you have to do is run it along the floor and your cat will not be able to resist the temptation to pounce on it. This game is the best ice breaker between you and your cat. Once your cat gets used to you and the surroundings, be prepared for him to fuss over you and play with you all the time.

a. Special Cases

There are some special cases when you, as an owner, have a larger responsibility towards your pet. If you have a dog, a resident cat or even a child in your house, the steps you take to introduce the cat will be different. As mentioned before, the Himmie has a certain pecking order that it prefers. Another unique case is when you adopt an adult Himalayan Cat. Here are some simple measures that you can take if you are wondering how you can make your Himalayan Cat feel more secure and comfortable.

Introducing your Himmie to your Pet Dog

The Himmie is unusually friendly with a dog. There are very few chances that your Himmie will dislike or get intimidated by your pet dog. However, you cannot say the same for your pet dog. Breeds like the Labrador or the Golden Retriever are natural care givers. So, they will not harm your cat without reason. In case you have a more aggressive breed, you might want to ensure that you take the following measures:

– In the beginning stages of the interaction, keep the dog and cat in separate rooms. The best way to ensure that they get used to each others' scent is to feed them on either side of the door of the room where the new cat is residing. If you feel like your dog is barking at or staring at the door or even scratching the door aggressively, don't force him to eat near the door. You can do simple things like switching the blankets of the pets or even placing the blanket of your cat next to the feeding bowl of your dog and vice versa. When the scent of the other animal becomes a regular affair, they will be able to eat comfortably on either sides of the door.

- Once you allow regular interactions on either side of the door, they will be comfortable to eat their entire meal. This is when they are ready for the next step of introduction.

- The next step is a face to face meeting of the two pets. Make sure these interactions are supervised and leashed. It is likely that your cat will get more comfortable with the dog first. When you are sure that the dog will not bite or manhandle your cat, you can let the cat loose while keeping the dog on a leash. Your cat will take his time to explore the possibilities of interactions with the cat.

- It is important for your dog to learn to obey commands. Special commands like 'Stay', 'Heel', 'Come' and 'Sit' must be familiar to your dog. If you have not trained your dog yet, make sure you start the process. You can also condition your dog to behave well with the cat by rewarding him every time he is well behaved with your cat.

- Irrespective of whether it is an introduction phase or not, never leave your cat and dog unleashed when there is no one at home. Unsupervised interactions can never be controlled entirely. Remember that your dog can kill your Himmie even with a playful bite. Especially if you are dealing with a kitten and a puppy, you must be very careful.

There is a level of compatibility between different cat and dog breeds. So, before you bring home a Himmie, make sure that your dog is going to be well behaved with the cat. If the breed of dog that you have at home is naturally aggressive, you must consult specialists and breeders before you bring home a cat. There are signs that show you how safe or unsafe it is for the two animals to interact. If your dog has ever tried to attack or snap at your new cat, it means that the compatibility is not great. A Himalayan Cat is not too aggressive. So you need not worry about hissing and scratching when your Himmie meets the dog for the first time.

You can ensure that there are no unpleasant and aggressive interactions by taking these simple precautions. Contrary to popular belief, dogs and cats make great friends. It is up to the pet owner to ensure that the initial encounters are safe and predisposed.

Your New Himmie and Other Cats

If there is already a resident cat in your home, expect the Himmie to become more dominant with familiarity. It is stressful to your old pet to deal with the fact that there is another cat in the house. Quite obviously, it is stressful for you as well to make sure that your pet does not feel neglected or out of place. You need to take each step at a time to make the situation more relaxed for you, your older cat and the your new Himmie.

- The first direct interaction should be scheduled over a weekend. This will make sure that you have all day to spend with the new cat and your resident cat. You can make sure that there are no unpleasant interactions. It is always best to have these interactions during meal time. You can expect some growling and hissing but it will not be entirely aggressive. To make sure that it does not get out of hand, you must place the feeding bowls at opposite ends of the room. Once the feeding is done, separate them instantly.

- Cats are territorial by nature. So make sure you establish the boundaries for both the cats. When your new cat is out of the confinement from its bonding room, you might want to make a special corner for him that is not too close to the existing space of your resident cat. Just place the feeding bowl and the cat bed in the designated area with your cat's favorite toys.

- The interactions between your cats must be gradual. You can try the blanket switching technique with cats as well. When they are accustomed to each others' scent, they become comfortable with each other. You must allow them to spend more time with each other slowly. Only when you are assured that they are relaxed in each other's company, you can leave them unsupervised. Until then you must never leave them unattended in the same space. This is especially true for nighttime.

- If you have more than one cat at home, you will notice that one of the resident cats will take the initiative to introduce the new cat to the existing group.

It is common for the cats to not get along immediately. If this is true for your resident cats and the new kitten, make sure you do not punish either of them. Just separate them when they get anxious. You must understand that this behavior is purely instinctive. With regular interactions, the cats will learn to live together peacefully.

Your Himmie and babies in the house

Usually, Himalayan Cats are very sensitive and tolerant towards children. But, when you have brought home a new cat, it is quite possible that the children will get too excited and actually scare the new cat. Children may squeal or wail when they see the cat. Now, a child also looks, behaves and smells very different from an adult. This unfamiliarity is not only distressing for the cat, it is also dangerous for your child. There are some rules to introduce your child to the new cat.

- Make sure your cat and the child have regular interactions. At no point will you let the child venture alone into the bonding room of the cat. You can teach your child to call the cat soothingly and even just watch the cat quietly until it gets accustomed to the presence.

- Scent is a very important thing in the world of animals. They relate to things purely on the basis of the smell. So it would be a good idea to let your child handle some of the cat's items so that the scent is left behind for the cat to get used to. You can give your child one responsibility like handling the blanket of the cat or even just filling up the water bowl.

- If you have a toddler at home, you cannot assign duties. It is a good idea to use the sock technique of introduction. All you need to do is rub a sock of the toddler on the cheek of the cat. Then, let the toddler wear the sock. Because of this rubbing off of the scent, the cat will trust the toddler as a friend that he can trust.

- Children must also be told that the cat is not a toy. You must constantly remind the child that pulling the ear or tail of the cat can be really painful for the cat.

Himmie owners swear by the tolerance of their wonderful kitties. They are very gentle and will often make great companions for children to play with. Most children and Himalayan Cats develop a very close bond that is simply beautiful.

a. Bringing Home an Adult Cat

Adult cats are very different from kittens. They will take longer to get used to the household and the people living there. Whether you have rescued or adopted an older cat, there are simple tips and tricks that will help you make the cat feel comfortable. Remember that an adult cat comes with several past experiences. His behavior will depend entirely on the kind of interactions that he has had with people in the past. You can do a little background check and make necessary adjustments in your lifestyle to accommodate an adult cat.

- You must make sure you ask your breeder or the owner of the pet rescue centre all the details of your cat's history. There may be specific toys that the cat is fond of. There may also be special scents or fragrances that the cat might require to feel comfortable. It is also important to know if your cat pet-to-be has had an abusive history. If yes, you must understand completely about the things that might make the cat anxious or uncomfortable.

- You can keep the adult cat in a cat carrier for a few days. In case there is a specific bonding room for the new cat, make sure you leave the carrier there. This can become your cat's permanent hideout and also zone of comfort.

- The litter box, food and water must be introduced to the new adult cat. Place them all in the bonding room or confinement room of the cat.

- When your cat is ready, you can take him/her to new parts of your home. It is absolutely mandatory that you familiarize the cat with all areas of your home. For an indoor cat like the Himmie, being able to look for resting spots and hiding spots becomes possible only when he is comfortable with all the space available.

- With an adult cat, conditioning becomes necessary. You must make time to play with the cat, talk to him and just be around him. A Himalayan Cat requires more attention than other cats and you must try as hard as you can to keep him happy. Only when the cat is sure of you as the right companion will he open up and be friendly.

- Make sure you keep an eye on your new cat. If he does not eat properly or use the litter box, you might have to seek some help from an expert. Another common problem with adult cats is the development of skin problems. These are all signs of discomfort and unhappiness in the cat.

With a Himalayan Cat, it is easier to overcome these special requirements. This is why it is considered the ideal pet for people who need constant companionship.

Chapter 7: Things To Know Before You Buy a Himmie

There are several cat breeders who will help you find the right Himalayan Cat for you. When you are looking for a new Himalayan Cat, there are two options available for you: Buying a Himmie or Adopting a Himmie

Things to consider when buying or adopting

You will be able to find several Himalayan Cats for sale. Whenever you are planning to bring home a Himmie Kitten on sale, make sure you talk to your breeder about the personality of the cat that you are looking for. He will be able to find the right Himmie Kitten that will suit your requirements. When a breeder recommends a certain kitten, they will keep in mind the temperament and the attitude of the parent cats to determine the personality of the kitten. Since these breeders also stay with these cats from the time they are born, they watch and understand how they behave with people. When you are buying a Himalayan Cat, there are some things that you must consider:

- **Life Span-** The ideal lifespan of a Himalayan Cat should be between 9-13 years. Check with your Himalayan Cat breeder about the history of your cat to understand the history of the kitten's parents and their life span.

- **Temperament of the Cat-** Although Himmies are known to be of a very gentle temperament, you must enquire about his/her social skills. He/she will most probably take after his/her parents and his/her behavior will be similar to theirs.

- **Older Cat or Kitten:** This is a question that you will definitely face when you are looking at buying a new cat. Himalayan Cat rescue homes and adoption centers will help you find a suitable adult cat. However, if you are looking at raising a cat, you may want to get yourself a kitten instead.

- **Cost:** A Himalayan Cat costs about $900. However, the breed plays a very important role in determining your Himalayan cat's price range. If your cat comes with a pedigree certificate, it could cost you up to $1200. Of course, if you decide to adopt a Himalayan Cat, you will get your cat for free.

- **Does your cat need a friend?** Research shows that cats that grow up in pairs are the happiest. So, if you want to get your cat a companion, you can ask your breeder for the most suitable option. The best companion for a Himalayan cat is another Himalayan cat.

- **How pet friendly is your home?** A Himmie is the perfect apartment cat. So even if you live in an apartment, it will not really matter. However, if there are any restrictions with respect to keeping pets in your apartment, you must be aware of it. In addition to that you must make sure that you also have access to pet stores and vets in the area that you live in. If you feel that your home is inconvenient for your pet, you might want to rethink the option of owning a cat.

- **Your Lifestyle-** If you feel like your Himmie will not have enough company while he is at home, do not even think of purchasing a cat. Himmies crave attention and can have several health complications if they are not given ample love and affection.

Once all these issues have been sorted, you can prepare your home for the Himmie. There are several Himmies that require a home. You can consider the option of adopting. However, before you do, here are some things that you must be able to provide your adopted pet with:

- Necessary care in case of reported abuse

- Vet assistance if he/she is ill or old

- A separate room or enclosure to protect him and other pets at home

- Constant care to help him adapt

- The necessary nutrition if he has health issues.

If you are confident of being able to provide all of the above, adoption is the noblest thing that you can do for your pet. Give him a loving home where he will be able to learn to live a life of dignity and happiness.

Chapter 8: Grooming Your Himmie

Himalayan Cats come with short fur, which is the deepest shade of black. The coat of a Himmie has a very leathery appearance. For a cat whose coat is his trademark, it would not be too surprising if grooming was expensive and time consuming. Now, what makes the Himmie even more special is the fact that his grooming requirements are almost zero. This is one of the most easy to maintain breeds of cat. All you need to worry about is overall hygiene and your Himmie will look more beautiful by the day.

a. Grooming essentials for a Himalayan Cat

As mentioned before, the grooming required for a Himalayan Cat is minimal. So, it is possible to maintain your cat with the bare essentials of cat grooming. They include:

Nail Trimmer:

A nail trimmer is the cheapest grooming tool that you can get for your cat. It will cost you under $10. This is a very simple tool to use. The reason most cat owners make use of these nail clippers is to ensure that the upholstery and furniture in the house is protected from the sharp claws of the cat.

There are several types of clippers that are available on the market. The safest ones are the cat claw scissors that come with blunt ends to protect the cat from cuts and clipping injuries.

Brushes and Combs:

There is a large range of brushes and combs that you can choose from for your cat. Usually, Himalayan cat owners pick fancy brushes to groom their cat. However, a brush is never as effective as a good comb. You may use a brush just to take of the stray hairs.

You can get your Himmie a slick brush that has steel bristles. These brushes not only keep the fur neat, they also massage the skin of your cat. This type of brushing action is loved by all types of cats, especially the Himmie.

You can also bring home grooming pads and gloves made of rubber. You can remove any dead hair for the short coat of your beautiful Himmie. You can even use flea combs to serve this purpose.

Toothbrush:

Dental Care is very important for cats. It is almost as important as it is in humans. The truth is that cats tend to have huge amounts of tartar deposits on their teeth. This may result in gum damage and even tooth decay. Instead of taking your pet to the vet for cleaning procedures, you can simply keep a brushing kit to keep your cats teeth in the best condition possible. If you do not maintain your cats dental health, there are chances that you will end up spending close to $500 on the anesthesia, antibiotics and other medicines required.

b. Grooming Tips

The Himalayan Cat is one of the most glamorous breed of cats. Just like its Persian parent, the coat of the Himalayan cat is not too easy to maintain. You have to dedicate time and put in a lot of effort to ensure that your cat's fur looks neat and shiny and not messy. Here are some tips that you can keep in mind to ensure that your Himmie is well groomed:

- Brush the hair of your cat regularly. Mats and tangles are common with Himalayan cats and you can get rid of these only with a Greyhound stainless steel comb.

- You may keep the fur short in the warmer months. However, this is not an act that your cat will consent to. A Himalayan cat is never pleased with the idea of getting his gorgeous locks trimmed.

- The area beneath the eyes must be washed everyday to prevent tearing of the eyes.

- Check the ears regularly. Any redness of irritated skin is the sign of an infection.

- Keep his nails trimmed.

- Use a vet approved toothbrush and toothpaste to keep your cat's dental health at its best.

Your cat must be introduced to these grooming activities right from the time he is a kitten. That way, he will not resist them when they become a routine. Introducing an adult cat to a grooming routine is challenging and might even require help from experts.

c. Does the Himmie Need a Bath?

Like any other cat, even the Himmie requires a good bath to help remove all the dust and dried skin from its coat. For a cat like the Himalayan cat that has a thick and long coat, bathing must be a regular affair. You must make sure that he is bathed at least once a month. It is essential, however, to wipe or wash the face of the cat every day.

Why does your Himmie need a Bath?

Cats usually give themselves a good clean up and keep their coat spotless by licking off all the dirt. If you observe your Himmie, you will notice how he constantly prunes and grooms himself all day long. So many pet owners argue that their cat does not require a bath regularly. However, this is not true. There are several reasons why your cat may require a bath:

- It is necessary to keep his coat clean and free from ticks and fleas.

- The amount of oil on the skin is reduced.

- Your kitty will smell pleasant if given a good shampoo and bath.

- He might have soiled himself in the kitchen or litter box.

- They tend to climb up chimneys and really soil themselves.

- A vet may recommend a bath to help your cat recover from specific health conditions.

- It gives you an opportunity to really bond with your cat.

Things you must keep handy

When you are giving your cat a bath, remember that you cannot leave him unsupervised for even one second until he is ready to be wrapped in a towel and dried up. So, you must keep all the necessary supplies handy to avoid having to walk in and out of the cat's bathing area. The best way to ensure an uninterrupted bath is to make a checklist of all the necessary supplies. Here is a quick look at the things you will need to give your cat a bath:

- Cat Shampoo

- A pitcher or spray nozzle to rinse the cat

- Rubber Gloves to prevent injuries to the cat because of your nails

- Cotton balls to clear up the ears

- A large towel to dry him off

- A small towel to just clean his face

Giving your cat a bath

Most people choose to give their cats a bath in the tub. This is not the best option as bending over the tub can really strain your back and give you a hard time. It is a much better idea to either use a small basin or even the sink in your bathroom. Cleaning up afterwards will also be easier when you choose this option. You can follow step by step instructions to give your cat a bath that is painless and relaxed.

- Fill the tub or the sink with warm water. You must make sure that the water is not too hot or too cold. The water must be 2 or 3 inches deep if you have an adult cat. For a kitten just an inch depth will do.

- Avoid a faucet or a jar to pour water on the cat. He will never appreciate it. You can gently wet the cat and then make a good lather with the shampoo.

- You must treat your cat's coat in the same way as you would treat your own hair. You must rinse the shampoo off gently and make sure that it is entirely gone. Leaving traces of the shampoo on the coat might lead to unwanted infections.

- During the entire bathing process, prevent splashing water on your cat's face. Cats simply hate this. Instead, you can just use a damp wash cloth to wipe the face and clean the ends of the cat's mouth.

- To clean the ears of a cat, just use a soft cotton ball. Never put objects like a Q tip or other pointed objects in to the cat's year. Even a slight squirm or nudge can cause serious injuries to your cat.

- When you are done bathing him, cover him with a large towel. Dry off as much water as possible. With a little rubbing with the towel, your cat will be fully dry.

When you give your cat a bath, make sure you use a good cat shampoo. In case you run out of it and don't have time to go to the pet store, you can just use a baby shampoo. Never use any cleaning product on your cat as it will irritate the skin and eyes.

d. Brushing your Himmie

The Himmie is a short-haired cat. Therefore, owners neglect the brushing aspect of grooming as the fur will not get matted or tangled. But there are several benefits of brushing your Himmie regularly. Unlike a long haired cat, you will not have to do this every day. However, a good, thorough brushing once a week will help:

- Improve blood circulation

- Add more sheen to the already gorgeous fur of your Himmie

- Remove loose hairs, if any

- Remove dried skin to keep the fur healthy

- Remove parasites, if any.

How to Brush the Fur of your Himmie

Brushing may seem like a very ordinary task. However, if done right, the benefits of brushing your Himalayan Cat will be multiplied. If you look up any blog or book with Himalayan Cat information, brushing is suggested as a great grooming technique. Here is how you can brush the fur of your Himmie, the 'right' way:

- Make sure all the strokes are even and in the direction of the fur. This will help eliminate the loose hairs and actually massage the cat's body.

- Using a cat hair brush, brush off all the loose hairs for your cat's body.

- You can even use your grooming gloves to get rid of any debris that is visible on your cat's coat.

- Your cat's skin consists of several natural oils. Massaging the body thoroughly after brushing will help distribute this oil evenly across the cat's body to produce healthier and shiner fur.

- Your cat's skin is very thin. So make sure the bristles of the brush are not too sharp. You must also ensure that you do not apply too much pressure while brushing the fur. It can cause cuts and bruises more easily in a short haired cat like the Himmie.

e. Controlling Shedding

Shedding is a common problem with the Himalayan cat. It is a common process by which the cat loses the dead hair. In an indoor cat like the Himalayan cat, shedding is not a seasonal affair. It will occur all year long. If left unattended, you will notice cat hair everywhere. From the furniture to your wardrobe, your cat's hair will make its way to all corners of your home.

Regular grooming is one of the best ways to minimize shedding of your cat's fur. While shedding is not a medical problem per say, there are some special cases when you must alert your vet about the shedding of your cat's hair. Shedding is a matter of grave concern when:

- Bald patches begin to appear on the skin

- Your cat obsessively scratches or licks a particular area

- The amount of hair loss is a lot more than usual.

In such cases, shedding might be due to:

- Ringworm infections

- Allergies

- Infection by bacteria

- Fleas
- Hormonal problems
- Prescribed medication
- Stress
- Imbalanced diet
- Poor grooming and hygiene
- Pregnancy

If there is a medical cause for the shedding, your vet will be able to provide you with the necessary remedy. Once this course of treatment is over, you can follow some simple steps to keep your cat's shedding under control.

- Keep an eye on the cat's skin when you are grooming him
- Grooming regularly is necessary
- Make sure your cat gets a proper, balanced diet.

With these precautions, you will be able to take good care of the trademark fur of the Himalayan cat. It is recommended that you take your cat to a pet barber once every 6 months. While your kitty will resent it, this process will promote thicker, healthier and shinier fur.

f. Declawing

Many pet owners think of declawing as a suitable grooming technique. This is a surgical procedure that removes the claws of the cat entirely. Also known as onychectomy, this procedure involves the removal of the end bones of the cat's toes partly or entirely. This is a practice that is very common in North America. However, because of the effects it has on the cat and its well being, it is also considered animal cruelty in many parts of the world.

This practice is followed in order to prevent the cat from damaging furniture and property. Other pet owners also justify declawing a cat as a method of protecting other people from being scratched or hurt by their cat. In many apartments, people are not allowed to keep cats unless they are completely declawed.

It is quite certain that these people do not understand the seriousness of this procedure. It is not a way of keeping the nails trimmed or blunt. It is a medical surgery that has untoward repercussions for the cat. You see, the toenails of your cat are attached very closely to its bones. So, removing the claw is as good as amputating the toes of your cat. The period of recovery is extremely painful for the cat. There is also no guarantee that your beloved pet will recover entirely from this traumatic experience. For this reason, several European countries have strong laws against declawing the cat.

If you have considered declawing or even been suggested to go for it, remember that you are tampering with the beautiful design that is the cat's body. The toes and claws are an important part of the anatomy of the cat, which makes it more agile and graceful. You are also depriving your cat of its instinctive defense mechanism, in case it ever escapes to the outdoors. To help you understand better, here are some drastic problems that your cat will face during the period of recovery:

Physical Discomfort

- Remember that the cat will not lose its instinctive behavior even if it is in pain. He will still want to jump, scratch and even play despite the pain. You cannot put a cat in a wheelchair! He will also have to use the litter box. So, the time taken for recovery will vary with each cat.

- For up to 3 days, you will notice lameness in the cat. It will drag itself to go through with its routine.

- Almost 80% of cats that have undergone declawing have shown signs of complications after surgery. While the complications developed post surgery in some, others reported issues after release. These complications were caused due to wrong sheering techniques or even the blade used for surgery.

- The most common medical conditions include abscesses, necrosis of tissues, growth of deformed claws, motor paralysis, nerve damage, hemorrhage, bladder inflammation due to stress, infections, swelling and even reluctance to walk.

Behavior Changes

The Himalayan Cat is very peaceful and pleasant by nature. With declawing, however, several owners swear by the fact that the personality of the cat changes. There are valid reasons to support this change in behavior and personality of the cat.

- The biting frequency and strength increases in most cats. The only possible explanation to this is that when a cat loses one form of defense, it activates another.

- House soiling is twice as common in declawed cats. Firstly, they become reluctant to walk and put pressure on their paws. In addition to that, severe cases like nerve dysfunction and even lameness renders the cat quite helpless.

- Aggression is very common in cats post-declawing. The pain makes them more defensive against people. And the fact that you, as the owner, inflicted that pain upon him makes you less trustworthy in the eyes of the cat.

Almost 45% of cats that have been declawed are referred to vet teaching hospitals and cat schools to sort out behavioral issues. The change in behavior is more drastic if the cat has undergone tendonectomy in the process of being declawed. The repercussions of these behavioral changes include relinquishing cats to shelters. For a cat like the Himmie, which gets so attached to people, this experience is extremely traumatic.

Reasons not to declaw

By now, you must have understood how painful the experience of declawing is for your cat. Here is a brief list of the obvious reasons to avoid declawing of your cat:

- When you declaw a cat, you are actually maiming it. There are several emotional, behavioral and physical complications that result from declawing your cat.

- The claws of the cat are an essential part of its anatomy. Your cat requires its claws to stay mobile, to balance itself and to also defend itself from predators.

- The process of declawing is irreversible. By amputating the bone ends of the cat, you are subjecting it to potential disability. Secondary complications that come with this surgical procedure cannot be undone.

- Very rarely, contracture of tendons occurs due to declawing. This makes it difficult for the cat to walk properly. Cats tend to rest all their weight on their hind legs as their front paws are actually missing. This type of imbalance also makes the cat experience muscle atrophy.

- It is extremely stressful for a cat when he is out of balance. Like we all know, cats tend to jump off high counters, trees and even leap up to incredible heights. With a primary organ responsible for their ability to balance missing, cats tend to become very distressed.

- People who own Himalayan Cats disregard the need for a cat to defend itself. Although your Himmie may stay indoors for most of the day, what do you do if it accidentally gets out? By declawing your cat, you are making him entirely defenseless in an environment that is extremely hostile. The claws, sometimes, grow back after 15 years of declawing. Even then, it might be crooked and deformed. So with no chance of replacement, you are practically stripping your cat of its primary defense mechanism.

- Emotional distress is highly prevalent in cats that have been declawed. These cats become extremely insecure and troubled. The most obvious signs of being upset are urinating on a rug that you love the most or even knocking down an antique object. Cats become very hostile to people in general and will bite more often.

- One common habit of a cat is to scratch the sand in the litter box. When they are declawed, they will find this activity extremely painful. As a result, your cat will become averse to the litter box. They may find alternate places to do their business. If your cat develops this habit, you will find it extremely hard to break.

So, if you are still concerned about your cat's sharp claws causing damage to people and property, you can look for alternatives.

Declawing alternatives

- Trim your cat's nails with a nail clipper. This will reduce the damage caused by your cat's claws to a large extent.

- Another simple option is to provide your cat with a scratching post. You can attract your cat to the scratching post by using scent sprays that smell like catnip. A sisal scratch post is most recommended for cats as the roughness of the surface is just right for the cat to fulfill its urge to scratch something.

- One of the simplest and most effective solutions is Soft Paws. This is a nail cap made of vinyl that you can simply glue to the front claws of your cat. It is best recommended for those who have cats like the Himmie that spend most of their time indoors. You can even protect your children from the cat with the help of Soft Claws. What is best is that Soft Paws comes in a variety of colors as well if you want to experiment and give your kitty a nice manicure. Once these caps wear off, they can be simply replaced with a new set.

- Train your cat. That is the best way to protect your space and others from the claws of the cat. Teach your cat to only use the scratch post. You can also train it to be at its best behavior when it is around strangers.

For a cat like the Himmie, which remains indoors, all the above alternatives work fine. In case your Himmie is in the habit of venturing outside (not very likely), you might want to avoid clipping the nails or even using nail caps so that the kitty can be on guard.

g. Keeping your Cat's teeth healthy

Dental health is a very important part of your cat's overall health. With the Himalayan cat, especially in the flat faced variety, dental problems are very common. The structure of the jaw and the placement of the teeth can lead to periodontal diseases if proper care is not taken. Here are a few tips on how you can keep your cat's teeth sparkling clean:

- If you ever feel like your cat's breath is foul, don't assume that it is natural. This is a definite indicator of bad oral health. If you notice bad breath and drooling, there are chances that your cat has tooth decay or gum diseases.

- Get your cat's teeth checked annually. Your vet will be able to provide you with dental services for your cat. If there are any evident signs of oral issues, make sure you give your vet details. Never ignore even the slightest detail like bleeding of the gums after food, drooling and bad breath.

- You can have a routine to clean your cat's teeth regularly. Initially, your cat might resist this. However, you can start by cleaning your kitty's teeth with gauze or cotton before actually proceeding to a brush. To start with, you can just dip your finger in some tuna water and rub it along his teeth and gums to make sure he is conditioned to enjoy his brushing routines. When you begin to brush your cat's teeth, make sure you use specially created cat toothpaste.

- Occasionally massage his gums to ensure that you stimulate it. In case there are existing gum problems, massaging will help speed up the healing process. The gums of your cat also become stronger. The ideal color for your cat's gums is pink. If it is reddish, then this is a sign of infection and irritation.

- You can include a small portion of dry foods or raw meat to stimulate his chewing abilities. Make sure the portions are very little, for dental health only.

Make sure your cat's dental health routine is regular. You must never wait until the last minute. Dental procedures are extremely expensive and are also highly stressful for the cat.

Chapter 9: Watching the Health of Your Himmie

A Himalayan Cat breeder will tell you that the beautiful animal is actually very healthy by nature. It is not until its teens that you will notice health issues with the Himalayan Cat. It is always a good idea to have your breeder check your cat for ailments before you bring it home.

There are no real concerns with the health of the Himmie. However, since this is a 'man-made' breed, you can expect genetic issues. One parent of this cat, the Burmese cat is known for having several health issues and there is a good chance that some of these are passed down to the next generation or the pedigrees that are created.

It is a fact that all breeds of cats are capable of inheriting genetic problems, just like people. So if you have a cat breeder who does one or more of the following, make sure you look elsewhere:

- does not provide you with a health guarantee on the kittens

- tells you that your kitten is 100% free from health issues

- tells you that the kitten has been placed in isolation due to health concerns

There are a lot of facts that determine the health of your cat besides the genetic makeup. The most common reasons for health problems in cats include:

- Dry, cheap cat food

- Infections from external agents

- Irregular food timings

- Hostile environment inside the house

- Lack of exercise

- Lack of attention and care from the owner

If your cat is behaving abnormally, you must make sure that you have him checked by a veterinarian. Your cat will display obvious signs that will tell you that he requires medical attention. Here are 10 signs that you must look out for in your Himmie to ensure that he gets to a vet before things turn ugly:

- Sluggishness and shortness of breath

- Bad breath

- Blood in stool or urine

- Sudden weight loss

- Painful and swollen abdomen

- Chewing and licking of skin

- Choking

- Constipation

- Coughing

- Hostility towards owners and other people

The signs and symptoms vary with different disorders. However, with the Himmie, even one of the above signs is a matter of concern. You must take him to a vet right away to make sure that there are no inherited diseases.

a. Most Common Health Issues with the Himalayan Cat

There are four issues that most Himalayan Cat owners face:

- Polycystic Kidney Disease

- Watering of the Eyes

- Breathing issues

- Hairballs

We will discuss in detail the causes, symptoms, diagnosis and treatment of these disorders before moving on to other health issues that you must look out for in a Himalayan Cat.

1. Polycystic Kidney Disease

Polycystic kidney disease is a common health issue that is faced by the Himalayan cats. This condition can be extremely serious and in worst cases can also lead to the death of the cat if proper care is not taken.

A cat's kidney consists of certain tissues known as the parenchyma tissues. Sometimes, these tissues can be replaced by multiple cysts. These tissues are very important for the proper functioning of the kidneys of the cat. When they form cysts instead of getting differentiated, the condition is known as Polycystic Kidney Disease.

These cysts are sometimes filled with fluids or semi-solid substances. They may also enclose air within them. These renal cysts are usually found in the nephrons. Nephrons are the functional cells in the kidney that are responsible for the filtering process. They might also be formed in the collecting ducts present in the cats. Most often, these cysts infect both kidneys of the cat.

The condition itself is not life threatening. However, improper care can lead to rapid progression that can be fatal to the cat. Usually all breeds that have descended from the Persian cat are susceptible to polycystic kidney disease.

Symptoms of PKD

The biggest problem with PKD is that it cannot be detected in the initial stages. The cysts are not detected until they become very large. Sadly, the cysts are only detected when they become so many that they cause kidney failures in the cat.

The common symptoms associated with a progressed condition are lumpy kidneys and palpitations. The cat will experience a lot of abdominal pain, which will lead to severe muscle spasms and palpitations.

The problem with these cysts is that they do not cause any problem when they are in the initial stages; they do not cause any discomfort. However, they only become evident when they are almost life threatening.

Causes of PKD

In addition to the genetic factors, there may be several other contributing factors that lead to PKD. This is a common disorder that is seen in cats that have descended from Persian cats.

Of course, the condition is found in other breeds of cats as well. As a result, it is impossible to blame only genetics for this condition. There are several endogenous factors as well. One of the most common causal factors is hormonal imbalance. Hormones like parathyroid hormones and vasopressin, when not available in the required levels, can lead to cyst formations.

Diagnosis of PKD

The first thing that a vet will ask for when you take your Himmie for an examination of PKD is the history of your pet. This includes details like the onset of the symptoms mentioned above and also specific genetic information about your cat. Besides this, there are several medical procedures involved in the diagnosis of polycystic kidney disorder.

The first step is the evaluation of the body fluids of the cat. Needle aspirates of the kidney are taken to understand how the cysts originated. In case the diagnosis is not clear, abdominal ultrasounds can be required. Urine analysis and the examination of the fluids in the cysts can also be evaluated to understand the extent of the condition and also the causal factors of the condition.

The vet may also want to study a bacterial culture of the cysts to understand if there is any secondary infection. A blood test is also required in some cases.

Treatment of PKD

Removal of the cysts is not a possibility when they have reached a progressed level. Usually, the treatment procedure involves the prevention of the possible consequences of these cysts. The usual consequences include complete kidney failure or kidney infection. The liquid or the substance inside these cysts is removed at regular intervals to ensure that the volume of the cyst is under control. In addition to that, the pain is also minimized by reducing the size of these cysts.

In order to avoid secondary complications such as bacterial infection, it is possible to provide oral medication. However, once PKD reaches a certain stage, complete cure is not possible. However, with ample care, you can increase the life span of your beloved pet and also reduce the complications associated with this condition.

Precautions to take if your Himmie has PKD

Once your cat has been diagnosed with polycystic kidney disorder, it is mandatory to take your cat for monitoring every six months. This is to check for possible associate diseases like kidney failure, infection and increased discomfort.

In conditions where sepsis or bacterial infection is not observed, constant monitoring is good enough to make sure that there is no uncontrollable progression of this disease. It is necessary to continue with long-term prognosis if your cat is susceptible to kidney failure due to the extremity of the condition.

The biggest issue with polycystic kidney disorder is the fact that the actual cause of this disorder is not known. As a result, preventive measures and accurate treatment are also not possible. Although selective breeding has been recommended as a measure to completely eradicate this condition, it is impossible to say how successful this attempt will be.

2. Watery Eyes in your Himmie

In the Himalayan cat, watery eyes or epiphora is a common problem. Especially in the flat faced variety, the chance of irritation due to the long fur is possible. However, you cannot always relate the eye problems of your cat to its fur. Watery eyes are a more complex problem in cats and can be caused due to various reasons.

The abnormal flow of tears is also known as epiphora. This is a common condition in several breeds of cats and has been associated with distinct shapes of eyes. Sometimes, there are conditions that, like the turning in of eyelashes or eyelids, can be observed right from the time your Himmie was born.

Symptoms of Epiphora

The common symptoms of Epiphora include:

- Tear drainage
- Tear stains on the face
- Formation of ulcers in the cornea
- Sagging of the skin around the eye
- Regular discharge from the eye
- Irritation and redness in the eyes
- Inflammation in the eyes
- Constant squinting

If the condition is congenital i.e. by birth, chances are that the opening of the eyelid is abnormally large. This leads to too much exposure of the eyeball, causing continuous watering. In case of eyelid tumors, you will be able to see a very evident patch of skin on the eyelids. Although this condition is very rare in the Himmie, it is something you must keep an eye out for.

Causes of Epiphora

Watery eyes in cats are usually linked to other conditions that your Himmie has acquired. They include:

- Fracture of the facial bones

- Swelling in the area adjacent to the tear drainage system

- Tumors in the eyelids

- Infections of tumors in the nasal cavity, eyelids and the eye

- Any blockage or inflammation of the tear duct can cause inflammation and overflow of tears

- Lack of normal openings in the tear drainage system can cause water eyes. This is a congenital condition.

- Presence of extra openings in the tear drainage system

- In case there is an absence of openings between the tear drainage system and the nose, excessive tear formation is observed.

- Inflammation of the eyes

- Glaucoma is also prevalent in some cats with teary eyes. In case of glaucoma, the internal pressure of the eye increases tremendously, leading to the formation of tears.

Any disorder in the eye or the cornea leads to watering of the eyes. Sometimes, there is also a fair chance that your Himmie has developed infections when you took him out for a walk or just let him out of the door.

Diagnosis of Epiphora

In order to understand the possible causes of epiphora, your vet might request for a background check of your cat's activities before proceeding into actual diagnosis. It is absolutely mandatory to diagnose the causes for watery eyes thoroughly.

Radiographs are very useful in checking for lesions in the nasal cavity and sinus area. Sometimes, a contrast material is used to understand the different structures that might be present. Your vet may also recommend magnetic resonance imaging or computed tomography to get a clearer picture of what is leading to the watery eyes.

For laboratory analysis, the material produced inside the cat's eye is taken and tested. Sometimes, when your vet is unable to arrive at any conclusive diagnosis, he might recommend surgical examination.

If the suspected cause is a foreign body, there are two methods of diagnosis. The first one involves flushing the tear duct. The second one is the use of a fluorescent stain to check for foreign objects under a blue light. Once the condition has been discovered, suitable treatment options are recommended for your cat.

Treatment of Epiphora

- The most important step in the treatment of epiphora is the reduction of irritation in the cat's eyes. This can be achieved by washing the foreign bodies out from the tissues of the eye. In long haired cats like the Himalayan cat, the most common problem is the fur.

- In case of any primary eye disease like corneal ulcers and conjunctivitis, treating them will become priority.

- Lesions that are blocking the tear duct must be managed to allow the normal flow of tears.

- If the cause for tear formation is any physical abnormality in the eyelid, surgery is recommended. These procedures are quite straightforward and only involve tacking the lids into the required position.

- If the eyelashes are a problem, they are removed by cryosurgery.

- If tumors are present, they are treated quite aggressively. The primary fear with tumors is that they may spread into other areas in the head including the optic nerve and the brain.

Medications are suggested based on the causes for watering. These medicines range from painkillers to antibiotic ointments depending upon the assistance your cat needs to speed up the healing process.

Precautions to take if your cat has Epiphora

The recovery phase is very important. Even a little bit of negligence can result in a relapse of irritation and inflammation. It is recommended that you use an Elizabethan collar during the healing phase. In case of inflammation, your vet might ask you to bring your cat for revaluation once a week to check that the condition is completely fixed. If the problem persists, then you might have to improve the diagnosis efforts.

When surgical procedures have been performed, you must ensure that the dressing is checked regularly along with proper medication and cleaning. You must take your cat for regular checkups to ensure that there is no recurrence or relapse of the condition. Also, surgical procedures are subject to the risk of infections. So proper management of the wound and revaluation is an important part of the recovery phase.

3. Breathing Problems in your Himmie

The short fur on the Himalayan Cat is a very important cause of breathing difficulties. Respiratory issues have been observed in several short haired breeds including the British and American short haired cats. Medically, troubled breathing is known as dyspnea while rapid and short breathing is known as tachypnea. These difficulties, if neglected, can become life threatening for your cat. Therefore, it is necessary to have your cat thoroughly diagnosed if you observe one or more of the symptoms mentioned below.

Symptoms

Difficulty breathing

There is evident movement in the chest and belly while breathing

Nostrils flare open

The mouth is kept open to aid breathing

The elbows stick out from the body while breathing

The head and neck are stretched out in front of the body

Inhaling is difficult

Breathing is accompanied by loud noises

Fast Breathing

The mouth is open while breathing

Breaths are short paced and shallow

The pace is really fast

It is also common for cats to cough excessively when they have breathing difficulties. The treatment of breathing disorders is based on the causes of the problems. Here are some common causes of breathing issues:

Troubled Breathing

- Deformed nostrils

- Tumors or Infections in the nose, chest or mouth

- Elongated palate

- Allergic reaction

- Fluid accumulation in the lungs

- Toxins in the chest due to botulism

- Bloating of the stomach

- Blood accumulation in the chest region

Rapid Breathing

- Reduced levels of oxygen in the blood

- Anemia

- Asthma

- Accumulation of fluids in the lungs

- Accumulation of fluids in the area around the lungs

- Bleeding in the lungs

- Tumors

Diagnosis of Breathing Difficulties

Since the breathing difficulties in your Himalayan Cat may have several reasons ranging from tumors to infections, the need to diagnose the condition thoroughly is high. You must make sure that you leave no stones unturned in discovering the cause for breathlessness in the cat. Negligence in this area may have fatal consequences.

A diagnosis always begins with a background study of the cat to determine the incidents that may have preceded the condition. Diagnosis includes observation of the breathing patterns of the cat. The presence of heart murmurs is checked by listening to the chest. The color of the gums plays an important role in determining the reason for breathlessness. If the supply of oxygen is inadequate, the gums develop a bluish tinge.

There are some standard tests to determine the causes and symptoms of breathlessness in your cat. They include:

- Blood count

- Biochemical profile

- Urine analysis

- Blood test

These tests are useful in understanding if your cat is suffering from a low blood cell count. The presence of any internal infection can also be determined using these tests. The severity of the breathing disorder can also be determined using these tests.

Other tools used to diagnose breathing difficulties are ultrasound and x ray imaging. This is used to check the structure of the abdomen. In case there is a possibility of a heart disorder, your vet may recommend an ECG as well. Endoscopy is a common tool used to determine causes related to the airways or the nose.

Treatment of Breathing Disorders

The treatment depends entirely upon the cause of the breathing difficulty in your cat. In most cases, it is necessary to admit your cat to a hospital or a proper facility to provide the required amount of oxygen. Medication will be provided orally or intravenously to help the cat breathe better. Activity of the cat might be restricted until he has recovered completely.

Precautions to be taken

Cage rest might be recommended for your Himmie to get enough rest. Make sure you follow all the instructions given by your doctor. In case you observe any relapse in the breathing pattern, consult your doctor immediately.

4. Hairballs

One of the most unpleasant sights with long haired cats is that of them spitting out hairballs. The way the cat gags and snorts as it spews the hairball can break your heart. You cannot deny that you can keep your beautiful Himalayan cat away from the issue of hairballs. You need to take several precautions to make sure that hairballs do not turn into your kitty's worst nightmare.

They can cause intestinal infections that can be a major health threat to your cat. Now, it is impossible to prevent your cat from grooming himself. However, there are some simple measures that you can take to make sure that the occurrence of hairballs is controlled effectively.

Causes of Hairballs

The only cause of hairballs is the grooming routine that your cat carries out every day. Grooming and preening is a cat's second nature and there is nothing you can do to control it or stop it. Usually, when a cat licks itself, the loose hair that may be present will be picked up by tiny hook like structures present on the cat's tongue. Usually, the hair is able to pass through the digestive system. Sometimes, however, some strands stay back in the stomach and accumulate as the cat continues to groom itself.

You may have noticed that the problem of hairballs increases as your kitty grows older. This is because the grooming routine becomes more rigorous with age. In case your cat sheds fur too often, there are chances of hairballs being formed in the stomach. This problem is particularly common with breeds like the Himalayan Cat.

Symptoms of Hairballs

The most common symptoms are retching and gagging. However, there are some prominent symptoms that you will notice when hairballs are forming inside the cat's stomach:

- Lethargy

- Constant vomiting

- Sudden loss of appetite

- Diarrhoea

- Constipation

Preventing Hairballs

Of course, you cannot stop your cat from grooming itself. However, there are precautions you can take to ensure that the number of loose hairs is reduced:

- Make sure you groom your cat regularly. You must brush your Himalayan cat for at least 15 minutes each day. The loose hairs must be brushed off thoroughly to reduce the chances of strays.

- You can use cat food with hairball formula to reduce the retention of hair in your cat's stomach.

- You may give a recommended laxative to your cat to ease the process of digestion.

b. Other Health Problems that are common In Himalayan Cats

The three disorders mentioned above affect Himalayan Cats the most. However, there are several other external infections and prominent health issues that affect the Himalayan Cat. There are eight such disorders that your Himmie must be kept free from:

Skin Problems

For a long haired cat like the Himalayan cat, skin problems are quite frequent. There are several dermatological conditions that you must watch out for in your Himalayan cat. A common skin condition associated with the Himalayan cat is Seborrhea Oleosa where the skin turns red and leads to excessive hair loss.

Heat Sensitivity

Because of their long fur, these cats experience severe discomfort in heat. They will require air conditioning during the warmer months. You must never travel with your Himalayan cat when the temperatures outside are high.

Vomiting

Vomiting is a very common feline disorder. Cats usually vomit when they consume something poisonous. If your cat had been playing with a string or rubber band, for instance, there are chances that he might have swallowed it. In addition to consumption of inedible objects, vomiting can be a symptom of some form of infection, diabetes or even urinary tract diseases.

The symptoms with vomiting are quite obvious. You will find your cat breathing heavily and even drooling. The biggest health issue that follows vomiting is dehydration. Sometimes, your cat might not even be vomiting. It might just be regurgitation.

Therefore, you must take a sample of the vomit to the vet for thorough diagnosis and treatment.

Feline Lower Urinary Tract Infection

Almost 10% of cats are affected by Feline Lower Urinary Tract Infection. There are multiple causes for this disorder, which is actually a group of disorders that affect cats commonly. It is possible for both female and male cats to suffer from this disorder equally. It is most often stress related. In other cases, cats that eat dry foods might suffer from this condition. Feline Lower Urinary Tract Disorder is very common in cats that are unhealthy and overweight. It is possible for a cat in a multi-cat home to develop this condition due to territorial issues. The symptoms for Feline Lower Urinary Tract Disorder are:

- Too much strain during urination

- Traces of blood in the urine

- Urination in places that are unusual

- Loud Purrs and cries while urinating

- Constant licking in the urinary area to reduce the pain

- Depression

- Sudden Dehydration

- Loss of appetite

- Constant vomiting

The treatment for Feline Lower Urinary Tract Infection depends on the cause and the type of infection. The inability to urinate is a matter of great concern in pets. You must call your vet immediately if you observe one or more of the above symptoms.

Fleas

Fleas are not just an issue with dogs. They are very often seen in cats. In case of the Himmie, they are even more difficult to locate because of the color of the cat's fur. This is an external health issue that can be treated easily. The signs of a flea invasion include:

- Constant scratching of the skin

- Irritated and Inflamed skin

- Frequent licking

- Sudden Hair loss

- Visually prominent skin infections

If left untreated, fleas can make a home in your pet's coat for years. They cause anemia in cats if left untreated. Sudden weight loss and even loss of appetite are indications that your cat is being attacked by fleas. There are several powders, topical medicines and also foams that are available to treat fleas.

If the problem persists, it is best to see your vet for oral medicines to get rid of this condition permanently. Sometimes, the treatment is not restricted to the fleas alone. You might have to even treat your cat for skin infections and even eating disorders resulting from the presence of fleas in the skin for a long time.

Tapeworms

An internal infection by tapeworms can be hazardous to your cat's health. These parasites usually invade the intestines of cats and can grow up to 2 feet in length if left untreated. Tapeworm infections have very subtle symptoms. This is why you must always keep a close watch on your cat to ensure that the problem of tapeworms does not go undetected. The symptoms include:

- Sudden weight loss

- Vomiting

- Presence of small, white worms in the feces and in the anal region

The last symptom is the only sure shot way of saying if your cat really is infected by tapeworms. This problem is usually linked with the presence of fleas on your cat's coat. Ingesting a flea can result in an infection by tapeworms. It is important to handle fleas as well when you are tackling the issue of tapeworms. The most common modes of treatment include tropical medication, oral medicines and injections.

Diarrhoea

There are several reasons for cats to develop diarrhoea. In the case of the Himmie, the most common causes include:

- Liver disease

- Intake of spoiled food

- Allergies

- Ingestion of loose hairs

- Cancer

The symptoms of diarrhoea include loose stools. They are usually watery in nature. Diarrhoea can last for up to 6 months depending upon the causal factors.

The biggest problem with diarrhoea is dehydration. Therefore it is mandatory to give your cat plenty of fresh, clean water to consume. You must also reduce the quantity of food given to your cat for about 24 hours. If diarrhoea continues and is accompanied by loss of appetite, lethargy, bloody stools and fever, you must take your cat for evaluation by a veterinarian.

Eye Problems

Besides watery eyes, Himmies can suffer from several other eye problems. The most common infections include conjunctivitis, retinal infections, bacterial and viral infections. Glaucoma and cataract are age-related eye problems that need to be taken care of as early as possible.

The symptoms of an existing eye problem are:

- Cloudiness in the eyes

- Redness of the eyelid linings

- Deposits in the corners of the eye

- Tear stained fur

- Pawing of the eye

- Squinting

The preliminary treatment measures include flushing the eye with water and wiping off the deposits in the corner of the eye. If the problem continues, it is time to see your vet.

Your cat's health must be your priority. You can ensure that he stays in the peak of his health by taking him for regular vet visits, providing him with nutritious food and also ensuring that he gets enough exercise. Physical health issues can be treated quite easily. However, if you see sudden behavioral changes in your cat, it could be suffering from some psychological disorder. The following chapter discusses in detail the possible psychological problems that your cat might encounter and also effective ways to deal with them.

Chapter 10: The Psychology of the Himmie

The natural behavior of the Himmie is very easy to handle. They are extremely gentle and affectionate and make great pets. Of course, the Himmie is a cat that demands a great deal of attention. If you are unable to spend time with it, your cat will develop psychological problems.

You must understand that your cat also has mood swings and emotions that can go out of control. If you have observed a sudden change in the behavior of your Himmie, it can be linked to emotional stress.

Symptoms of Stress

With a well-behaved cat like the Himmie, it is very easy to notice the symptoms of stress. The most common symptoms include:

- Loss of appetite

- Reduced interaction with the members in the family

- Aggressive behavior

- Confinement to hiding places

- Elimination out of the litter box

- Too much grooming

- Change in interaction with other pets in the house

It is possible that your cat displays more symptoms of stress, including a change in voice. It is impossible to compare the symptoms seen in two different cats. The intensity of the symptoms varies from one cat to another. While in some cats the change is very drastic, some of them show such gradual progression that it is very easy to ignore. The Himalayan Cat loves to interact. So, you must always be alert to behavior patterns like excessive hiding to make sure that you do not allow the emotional distress in your cat to escalate.

What Causes Stress in Himalayan Cats?

There are several causes for stress in cats. Now, there are some factors that we do not even consider potent enough to cause dramatic changes in the cat's behavior. There are many changes in the immediate environment of the cat that seem ordinary for us. However, the impact that it has on your pet can be extremely damaging. These normal and usually overlooked causal factors include:

- Installation of new carpets

- Loud Music

- Change in the brand of litter

- Dirty litter box

- Inclusion of new furniture

- Visitors

- Repairs in the house

- Barking of dogs

- Appearance of strange cats or dogs around the house

- Travel

- Change in the brand of food

Then, there are some causal factors that are very evident as they have emotionally damaging effects on human beings as well. These factors include:

- Divorce

- Death in the Family

- Birth of baby

- Illness in the Family

- Abuse

- Inclusion of another pet

- Natural disasters

- Injuries

- Moving to a new home

Cats, as we have discussed in previous chapters, need to get used to the sights and smells around them in order to be comfortable. However, if you make sudden changes in your cat's environment, you can expect it to feel distressed. It is possible that over time, your cat will overcome these issues. If they persist, however, it is a good idea to consult an animal therapist. Even your regular veterinary doctor will be able to check your cat for emotional distress and provide you with necessary solutions.

How to Reduce Emotional Stress in Himmies?

When you see one or more of the signs mentioned above, the first thing you need to do is have your Himalayan Cat examined by a doctor. The reason for stress must be identified at the earliest. Although this is not easy, you can do a background check to come to suitable conclusions. The triggers for stress in your Himmie are not always evident. However, if you are aware of the sensitivity level in your cat, you will be able to determine the most obvious causes for stress.

It is important for you to understand that the hearing and smelling abilities of your feline companion are far more advanced than ours. Even the faintest sound or smell that is easily neglected by you is picked up by your cat quite easily. Scents from another cat, new smells inside the house like fresh paint, scents of new people etc. can be very stressful for your cat. So, if you are aware of any changes that have taken place around your cat's environment, you must include it in the list of suspected causes.

Here are some things that you can do to reduce stress in your cat:

- Prepare your cat for any big change that is impending.

- Have enough spaces in the house where your cat can rest or hide. If your cat does not want to be bothered, allow him/her to have a safe retreat.

- The litter box must be kept pristine. Try to keep the entire set up appealing to your cat. The location of the litterbox, the type of litter used and the number of boxes you include should be given a good amount of thought.

- If there are several cats in your house, and you notice tension and change in behavior amongst them, you need to make several modifications. You must make sure that every cat in your home feels completely secure in its environment.

- If your cat is getting too much attention from kids and visitors, keep him away from them. Even if the other pets in your home are giving him unnecessary attention, you should provide your cat with a space where he will be able to spend some time alone, in peace.

- Make sure you spend enough time with your cat. You must engage in interactive sessions and play with your cat to give him confidence. This is the only way you can develop a positive relationship with your cat based on affection and trust.

- Cats never appreciate change. So, try to make them minimal, especially with things that are associated with the cat directly, like his food, litter box and even water bowl. Any change around your cat must be gradual to help him accommodate it.

- Never leave the cat alone. If you are travelling, get someone to take care of your cat. Himalayan Cats, get extremely distressed when they are away from their owners even for a short time.

- The interactions that you have with your cat are extremely important to its emotional wellbeing. If you do notice stress in your cat, there is no need to be alarmed. All you have to do is give him as much time and affection as you can to help him get back to his old, playful self.

Chapter 11: Behavorial Problems That You Must Watch Out For

Himalayan Cats are furry, loveable creatures that are a pleasure to have as pets. However, like any other pet that we adopt, these Himalayan Cats also have some behavioral issues that you have to watch out for. These cats, which are mostly well behaved, by nature may need a little care from the owner's side to be a well behaved pet. But, these cats are not vicious by nature.

Let us first understand what the behavioral issues are that these cats are known to have. Listed below are some problems that have been identified to be common problems with Himalayan Cats.

Attention Seeking Disorder in Cats

Cats are known to 'meow' nonstop at certain times of the day or night. Their constant howling can become a nuisance for the owner. But before one jumps the gun and comes to the worst conclusion, it is sensible to sit down and understand what is causing your cat to behave in this particular manner. The howling of your cat can be broadly categorized as either crying or meowing. The cause for such behavior can be either emotional or physical pain that the cat is experiencing. Experts have noted that the attention seeking demeanor of the cats can be further classified as follows:

- Mournful howl: Some cats tend to howl in the night like they are calling out for help. This particular howl can make the cat owner cringe with sympathy for the poor creature. This mournful howl is mostly a result of deafness. In some cases this cry has been identified as the cat's cry for help in its old age. It is also associated with the insanity of an old cat.

The reason for this howl need not always be an emotional one. A certain condition called as Feline hyperesthesia is also associated with this behavior. When a cat howls during the night and is found to roll around in the house, you must consider this condition. This condition is commonly called Rippling Skin Disorder. This disorder is considered a stress disorder. However, the symptoms usually include a set of unrelated issues. The cats tend to become extremely sensitive to touch and the skin begins to show ripples. The possible causes of this disorder are: excessive presence of unsaturated fatty acids in combination with Vitamin E deficiency, brain infection or trauma or flea allergies. If the cat is diagnosed with this disorder then it is unlikely that it will be completely cured. So, paying attention to these issues can help you provide greater comfort to the cat and keep tabs on its behavioral issue.

- Chronic pseudo hunger: Hunger pangs are commonly observed in cats as well. Like human beings, cats also have food cravings that are unwarranted. Cats tend to develop a lot of liking towards some treats such as tuna flakes. This can also turn into an addiction of sorts. When you observe that your cat has been begging for food all day the reason is not hunger but pseudo hunger.

- The figure 8: Cats are known to run around their owner's feet in circles. This is also categorized under attention seeking issues of the cat. They are much like kids who need a little bit of extra attention. They also tend to rub themselves against your arm when they need extra attention.

- Meow chat: Cats are very vocal. They also like to have conversations with their owners. And, some chatty cats tend to prod their owners into lengthy conversations. If the owner refuses to spend enough time with the cat, then it tends to suffer from excessive loneliness.

- Scratching: Cats scratch. This is common knowledge. But, sometimes they overdo it and then the owner may have to be a little concerned. Excessive scratching can cause the cats to bleed from their skin. It has been noted that cats use scratching as a tool to demand for your attention. It is best to take note of this behavior before your beloved pet inflicts physical pain on itself.

Clawing to destroy

Cats are synonymous with clawing. They are known to scratch themselves, you and your furniture. But, when you realize that your cat is overdoing it, you might need a little help. If your cat is found to be clawing everything in its surroundings and causing damage to the valuables in your household, then considering some options such as training them not to do so or disciplining them in a friendly way should be considered. De-clawing is not an option to be considered though.

Litter Box being avoided

Owning a pet cat can be a nightmare if you wake up to find your house littered every morning. Cats by nature have no sense of where to or where not to litter. However, every cat can be trained to overcome this messy problem. Once you have understood that the reason your pet cat is dirtying your surroundings is not due to any sort of illness, suitable measures can be adopted to rectify this problem. The reason your cat is avoiding its litter box could be because the box itself is not hygienic and clean. If you have avoided your duties due to some unforeseen reasons and find yourself cleaning up cat mess, then, it is time to thoroughly clean the litter box.

Aggression towards other cats

When you see cats fighting amongst themselves, you will not consider it a big deal. This is especially true when you own more than one cat. But, it is wise to be watchful when your pets get into a fight. You have to ensure that the fight does not turn ugly. This brawl can have serious repercussions. Cats fighting is mostly attributed to fear, territorial understanding, stress venting or anxiety displays. There are various kinds of aggression that are seen in cats:

- Sexual aggression: Sexual aggression in animals is quite a common phenomenon. But, in cats it is not very commonly seen. However, when two cats get sexually aggressive towards each other, the dominating cat bites the victim cat's nape and there is an attempt to climb on the victim cat.

- Territorial aggression: This sort of aggression is also observed quite often amongst all animals. Much like dolphins, dogs etc. cats are also known to mark their territory. Cats urinate to mark their territory. The dominating cat is seen hissing, growling and readying himself to jump on his victim. Usually, the trespassing cat turns around respectfully and walks away. But, in some cases, the victim or the trespasser cat will put up a fight and things turn ugly. One interesting thing to note is: the cat which marks its territory need not be the oldest cat or the cat that has lived in the house for the longest period of time.

Aggression directed at human beings

It is unlikely that cats become friendly with everybody who visits your home. But, most of the domesticated cats are civil to guests. They will simply disappear from the scene if they are uncomfortable in the surroundings. However, when a cat tends to get aggressive towards people in general, it is a clear indication of the fact that the particular cat has been poorly trained when it was younger. Biting, scratching and unpleasant vocalization are indications of a badly trained cat. Some other causes of aggressive cat behavior towards human beings are listed below:

- Overstimulation: This problem surfaces when the owner of the cat does not understand the body language of the cat. There are cats that prefer petting while most prefer to be left alone. Even the most petting friendly cats do not like to be petted for unreasonable lengths of time. When they get over stimulated, they tend to scratch or bite to show that their petting session is over. If one closely observes, then, he/she will see that the cat starts pulling himself away, by pulling his ears back and by narrowing his eyes. If the owner fails to understand these signals, then, the cat begins to lash its tail. At the end, when the owner is simply being ignorant, then the aggression sets in.

- Redirected aggression: A cat's aggression towards his owner or other human beings may not necessarily be due to patting; sometimes, the sight of something disturbing can also result in aggression. When your cat spots a foreign cat or any other stranger animal around the house, then there is a possibility of the cat getting irritated by the sight itself. As a reaction to this, your cat will scratch or bite the first thing it can reach.

- Medical causes: This sort of behavior can also be a result of internal, undetected injuries or any other medical causes. This can range from hormonal imbalance to flea infestation. The cat expresses its distress through either biting or clawing dangerously.

Chapter 12: Training Your Himalayan Cat to Overcome Its Issues

Is your Himalayan Cat behaving in an undesirable manner and being a nuisance? Are you bothered by any of the behavioral issues that have been listed in the previous chapter? If yes, then here is a guide to how training your cat will help resolve these issues. Training your pet cat is an everyday process. Your cat has to be able to adopt these measures as a second nature. For this you will have to start the training process slowly in a firm yet friendly manner. Punishing your cat is not a solution to any of its behavioral issues. Cats are known for their ability to stay calm and loiter around in the house without making a mess of things. So, when you see such an unnatural event, it means that there is a serious problem that needs to be addressed through training.

Firstly, determine if the problem is behavioral.

Secondly, rule out possible medical causes that might be affecting cat behavior.

Lastly, if there is a genuine problem, take proper measures to set it right.

Some of the common behavioral problems that can be corrected by taking appropriate care are described below:

Avoiding the Litter Box

A well trained cat does not urinate outside of its litter box. So, when this happens and you have determined that it is a behavioral problem, you can take the following measures:

- Check the litter box and clean it if you have left it without appropriate cleaning.

- Do not make the cat smell its own pee as a punishment. This is nothing but bullying your pet and such behavior will serve no purpose.

- Check if your cat is stressed. Any change in its environment causes stress in them. They react very promptly to new family members, renovation of the house etc.

- If you find your cat taking a liking to a particular spot in the house, place the litter box in that area.

- Give your cat some more attention. This may be its way of attracting your attention as it has been missing your company.

Excessive scratching

Preventing the cat from scratching itself excessively needs you to be a more pro-active cat owner. Excessive scratching is a problem that is often observed in cats. Here are some measures you can take to prevent it from scratching itself.

- Do not resort to declawing.

- Trim the cat's claws carefully.

- Use diversion techniques. The most popular one being to create an alternate sound source that disturbs its scratching process.

- Apply a double sided tape on the spot that is being scratched regularly. Cats detest sticky surfaces.

- Whenever you find your cat indulging in scratching inappropriately, spray some water on its body or face. Do not drown the cat in water but spray the cat to divert him.

Aggressive behavior

Aggressive behavior towards humans, other cats or other human beings can be mitigated by taking certain steps in this direction:

- Create diversion through loud sounds. Clapping or any other such sudden sound can cause the cat to shift its focus.

- Ensure that your cat's atmosphere is not disturbing him or making him anxious.

- Do not throw yourself into the cat fight and try to separate the two animals that are fighting. This might result in you being seriously injured.

- Do not hit your cat or shake him when he is aggressive. Such behavior on your part will only add to his aggression.

All this needs an ample amount of patience. Ill-treating your pet is no way of disciplining him. If you are unable to handle your cat's behavioral issues, consult a vet and take their suggestion. This will guarantee marked improvement in his behavior.

Chapter 13: Is your Himmie Obese?

Himalayan Cats usually weigh up to 12 lbs in their adulthood. Since the Himalayan cat is not a particularly active cat, the food that he eats needs to be well balanced and also controlled. If you do not take good care of his diet, there are chances that he will become obese or overweight.

A plump kitty may sound nice and cute. However, for medium sized cats like the Himmie, the effect that they have on the cat's health and wellbeing are always negative. Besides usual problems like sluggishness and lethargy, obesity in cats has several associated health disorders.

Himalayan Cats are also indoor cats. This means that they need constant stimulation to keep themselves active. If your cat is unable to get the amount of exercise that he/she requires, be prepared to deal with 'weighty' kitty issues.

a. How to tell if your Cat is Obese?

Sometimes, it becomes very difficult to determine if your cat is, indeed, overweight. The level of activity and the agility seems to be just fine. So, cat owners think that they have a happy and fat kitty. But, there are sure shot ways of telling if your cat is becoming obese. You can try three simple tests at home before you have an actual expert test your cat for obesity:

- Feel the area around the rib cage of your cat. If you are still able to feel the rib cage through his fur, it means that he is still not obese. However if you have to press really hard to get to his rib cage, it means that your cat is heavier than the normal, acceptable weight.

- There is a distinct shape in a cat's waistline. The body tapers from the belly towards the hind quarters. If it is too stubby and even, it is a sign that your cat needs to lose weight.

- A hanging pouch between the hind legs of a cat is a definite indication of the cat being overweight.

Like humans, cats that are overweight will experience several health issues. Therefore, you must take the necessary measures to slim down your cat and maintain a healthy weight.

b. Health disorders in Overweight Himalayan Cats

One of the most common complaints in veterinary clinics across the globe is health disorders related to obesity. The biggest threat to the wellbeing of cats is feline diabetis mellitus. The second most prevalent disorder in cats due to obesity is hyperthyroidism, which is due to excessive production of thyroid.

According to experts, the chances of an obese cat becoming diabetic are double in comparison to cats that have a normal weight. This risk becomes 8 times higher if the cat becomes severely obese. The association between obesity and diabetes is quite evident. When your cat becomes obese, there is a drastic increase in the amount of inflammatory markers and oxidative stress. This causes insulin resistance, which leads to obesity.

The resistance to insulin is one of the most common problems found in cats. It has also been observed that a change in the diet is not as effective in increasing insulin sensitivity as the actual reduction in weight.

There are several other health conditions that can be found in cats due to feline obesity:

- Osteoarthritis and lameness - This condition occurs because there is too much stress on the medium sized frame of your cat. You will be able to hear loud thuds when your cat jumps off a table or chair, which indicates a gradual loss of agility in the cat.

- There are several skin problems like dermatoses as the cat is not able to groom itself properly. It is not agile enough to reach all the spots on his body.

- Too much pressure on the liver also causes liver problems like feline lipidosis syndrome.

- Urinary tract disorders are common in cats that are obese.

The biggest issue with obesity is not the condition itself. The inability of many owners to recognize this condition and provide necessary treatment is the cause for the drastic increase in feline obesity in the last couple of years. There are many cases that have been reported where owners are just used to over-feeding their cat. They actually find a normal sized cat malnourished and unhealthy.

As the owner, it is your responsibility to evaluate the condition of your cat's body on a regular basis. You can also get a body condition score to check for the amount of fat present in your cat's body. These scores show the difference in the calorie intake of your cat and the actual energy requirement. If your cat is being overfed, the score will increase to indicate an increase in fat deposits.

c. Tackling Obesity in Cats

It is not very difficult to maintain normal body weight. All you need to do is ensure that the width of the hips and shoulders are maintained without any visible bulge on the sides. You must also make sure that the belly of your cat does not hang too low. Since the Himmie is a slender cat by nature, fat deposits become very visually evident. There are a few things you can do to reduce obesity in your cat:

Understand what the right amount of food is

The amount of food that you give your cat should be just enough to keep them healthy. It is impossible to put a number on the amount of food that you should give your Himmie. However, you can measure the calorie intake in your cat. He will require about 55 kilocalories per kilo of body weight. So, Himmies will need close to 250 kilocalories each day.

Depending on your cat's health, you can determine how much food he requires. If there has been any recent surgical procedure or neutering, you must make sure you reduce the food intake accordingly. Free choice feeding is a very common problem among cat owners. They provide their cat with a range of flavors and choices, leading to overeating. If you mix dry cat food with canned food, there might be chances of overeating. Constant change in the taste makes your cat overeat because of novel tastes that he/she is able to experience.

Use a measuring cup to ensure that your cat is neither over fed, nor under fed. If you prefer free choice feeding, divide the food into two portions. Give your cat one helping in the morning and one in the evening. You must also be very careful that the feeding is age appropriate. Depending on whether you have a kitten or a senior cat in your household, the choice of diet will vary.

Keep your Cat Hydrated

You must make sure that there is plenty of fresh water available for your cat, especially if you are feeding him/her dry cat food, While most dry foods work very well for cats, lack of water might lead to issues like urinary tract disorders and also lowered kidney function.

Water is an essential nutrient for your cat. Irrespective of whether you are feeding him wet or dry food, you must give him enough water. The presence of adequate amounts of water in the body will help your cat assimilate the food that he has consumed. Proper digestion and elimination, which is the key to good health in a cat, is regulated by the amount of water available.

Give your cat a Low Fat Diet

The Himmie is quite an active cat by nature. Unfortunately, if he becomes obese or overweight, you will notice an evident reduction in his activity levels. For an indoor cat, who is not very active, a low fat diet is mandatory.

If you have put your cat on a weight loss diet, you must give him adequate amounts of protein. It is true that the calorie intake must be restricted. However, you must always make sure that you do not reduce the amount of essential nutrients. When you increase the amount of proteins, weight loss is aided while keeping the lean body mass intact.

Keep a check on the treats

If you are concerned about the health of your cat, make sure you reduce the amount of treats and tidbits. This practice must be extended to at least a couple of weeks after the 'diet' period. You must make sure that everyone in your family is aware of this rule. If you try and cheat out of affection, remember that you are harming your cat's health. It would help, instead, to cut your cat's meal down to smaller, more frequent meals. This will ensure that he does not experience hunger pangs while continuing to stay on a healthy diet.

Say No to crash diets

Crash diets are harmful for cats and they are harmful for humans. You must never starve your cat. In fact, no matter what restrictions you make in his diet, it must be supervised by a dietician. If you do not keep tabs on the amount of minerals and vitamins your cat is getting, it can lead to a fatal condition called hepatic lipidosis, which affects the liver.

Keep the activity levels high

Exercise is extremely important in cats. You cannot control the health and weight of your cat by merely altering the diet. You must ensure that he has an active lifestyle. While controlling the calories he takes in, you must also make sure that he burns the calories through exercise and activity. Here are some things you must do to make your cat's environment stimulating and engaging:

- Set aside a dedicated time to play with your cats. You can use simple toys like strings to help your kitty play and get a good workout.

- Allow his natural instincts to take over. You must let your cat climb, scratch and even chase around the house, These exercises are interesting to him, by nature, and will increase the process of weight loss.

- Get a feeding ball to give your cat one meal in the day. The advantage with the feeding ball is that your cat will have to put in some amount of effort to roll the ball and get to the food inside.

- The food bowl of your cat can be placed on top of a flight of stairs. This will encourage him to climb to get to the food.

-Try to take your cat outdoors as often as possible. A breath of fresh air will do you and your kitty a great deal of good.

Throughout the process of weight loss, you must be extremely patient. It will take several weeks and even months for your cat to lose weight. If you find it too hard to maintain the weight of your cat on your own, you can ask your vet for tips. You can even enroll in a veterinary weight loss clinic for additional support and information.

Chapter 14: Finding a Good Vet

You will find a lot of Himalayan Cat 101 online. In any case, it is necessary for you to have a reliable vet who you can trust with your pet. It is never a good idea to constantly change the vet who treats your Himmie. Cats, as you know, do not appreciate change. They are usually reluctant to cooperate with vets. So, you must give your cat time to get accustomed to the touch and voice of one vet. Once he/she is comfortable with him or her, your cat will be more relaxed during vet visits. A vet is an important part of your cat's life and you must make sure you look for the perfect one to take care of your pet.

There will be several large and small veterinary clinics around your town. Therefore, it can be quite confusing when you set out to choose one for your precious pet. The best way to look for a vet is to ask for recommendations from your friends and neighbors. If you know people in the neighborhood who have had pets for a long time, they will be able to recommend someone to you.

You must make a conscious effort to look for someone who is specialized in cat care. This section of veterinary care is growing rapidly and you will definitely find someone in the vicinity.

In order to be prepared for an emergency, here are some things that you might want to consider before you zero in on one vet:

- How far is your vet from your home?

- Is the commuting time too long?

- In case of an emergency, will you make it on time to the vet?

- Is the ambience of the clinic feasible for your cat?

It is always better to find someone close to your house. It must not take more than 15 minutes to drive to your vet. Even if it is not an emergency, remember that your cat is not particularly fond of long drives. Once you have found someone who seems to fit into all the requirements, you can make a trial visit. The chemistry between your cat and the vet is extremely important if you want to make it a long-lasting relationship. There are some signs that will indicate how comfortable you and your pet will be in a particular clinic. Make the following observations if you are visiting for the first time:

- The waiting room must be well maintained.

- The ambience must be comforting for the cat so that it feels secure when it is being examined

- If it is a common clinic for dogs and cats, how are they maintained when they are admitted for hospital care? Are they kept in separate cages?

- The people at the reception must be friendly. These people are going to be your point of contact in the coming sessions and you must be comfortable with them.

Once you are in the examination room, check how the vet interacts with pets and their owners. The tone must be soothing. He must be able to provide undivided attention to your cat. The vet must value your opinions about your cat's health and must be respectful towards you.

The personality of your vet plays an important role in the way he/she interacts with the animals. They must be genuinely passionate about their job. Without passion, you cannot be assured that they will go to all lengths to ensure the best for your cat. The vet must be good with cats and must have complete knowledge on the different practices and techniques that have evolved in veterinary practices. They must also make a conscious effort to upgrade their skills and knowledge.

Once you are assured of the behavior of the vet towards you and your cat, you need to get down to the technical and legal aspects:

- Is the facility adept in handling emergencies?

- How many cages or rooms do they have for the pets that have been admitted there?

- Is every staff member educated?

- Is the facility licensed?

- What are the costs of tests and surgeries?

- Is the pricing competitive enough?

- What are the insurance policies that they accept?

- How many emergencies are handled after regular working hours?

- Who takes care of the pets when they are hospitalized?

- Are they open to alternative medicines and treatments?

Once you have received satisfactory answers to all the above questions, you can be assured that this facility is best suited for your cat. Remember, the person you choose as your vet is going to be your partner in the wellbeing of your beautiful Himmie.

Preparing your cat for a vet visit

Taking a cat to the vet is not easy. If you ask other pet owners, they will tell you that it is definitely not the picnic that you expect it to be. Unknown to most people, cats experience a lot of stress when they are travelling. As a result, it is best that you prepare your cat well for a visit to the vet. Here are five tips that will make the visit less stressful for your cat:#

1. Create a pre vet routine

Even cats require a good amount of mental preparation before they are taken to the vet. Start by giving your cat a thorough check up from his head to toe. This can only be an imitation of the actual test that will take place in the vet's clinic. The idea is to get the cat used to being handled by the vet.

Getting your cat used to the carrier is another way to make the visit less stressful. If your cat learns to associate the carrier with vet visits, he might resist the visit. On the other hand, if you create associations like playtime or even outdoor visits with the carrier, your cat might look forward to the positive activities and be less stressed. You can designate the carrier as a nap place. Throw his favorite toys and treats inside the carrier to attract him towards it.

Of course, the actual travel to the vet is going to create a great deal of stress for the cat. You can reduce this by being affectionate to him during the drive. Play with him and pet him on the way keep his anxiety levels down.

2. Make your car cat friendly

Most cats dislike cars. So most of the resistance to the visit to the vet is not the clinic itself, it has more to do with the journey to the vet. Usually, cats are taken out in the car only during their visit to the vet. As a result, they automatically associate cars with the negative experiences that they might have had at the vet, including injections and bad tasting medicines. So cats can never stay calm and relaxed inside a car.

However, you can help your cat to make positive associations by including drives in the car in your daily routine. You can take the car for short distances too. Take the car to the park, for instance. Then your cat will stop making negative associations. You can even stop by at the vet's clinic for 5 minutes to get your cat used to the staff there.

The basic idea is to get your cat used to the car. He must learn to be calm and relaxed during these visits. Keeping some toys in the car and allowing him to play during these drives will also help a great deal.

3. Beat the waiting room blues

One place dreaded by all animals is the waiting room at the clinic. There are several unpleasant sounds like the barking of dogs and even chatter of humans that increase the levels of anxiety in a cat. Cats are, by nature, solitary animals and do not like being introduced to so many strange sights and sounds at one go. The best thing to do would be to leave your cat in the carrier until he is called in for examination. This gives him a secure hide out and he will be more at ease.

Make sure that the carrier that you are using is large enough. Place a nice cat bed or a cushion inside for him to rest on. You can also leave toys and goodies inside the carrier. A top loading carrier is a must as it will become impossible for you to get your frightened kitty out of a front loading one. Special pheromone sprays are available to reduce anxiety and stress in cats during their visit to the vet. These sprays imitate the scent that cats leave when they rub themselves against the legs of their loved ones.

You can also schedule your appointments to the less busy parts of the day. That way, the chaos in the waiting room will be lesser, making your cat feel more relaxed.

4. Get friendly with your vet

It is good to allow your vet to spend some time with your cat and break the ice. Of course, the vet is going to poke and prod the cat for examination. This becomes less stressful if the cat can look at the vet as a friend rather than a stranger. Make sure you clear up all queries related to your cat's wellbeing when you visit your doctor. Even if it means additional visits, do not shy away from it.

5. Send items from home for overnight stays

If your cat is due for overnight hospital care, send his favorite items from home. The idea is to keep him around familiar scents so that he does not get too anxious. There are several routine procedures like neutering that can be extremely stressful for your cat. However, making regular visits and sending him things from home can really help him to overcome this anxiety.

You must always work with your vet to ensure the complete wellbeing of your cat. You must trust the knowledge and expertise of your vet if you want him/her to be the best care giver for your cat. Usually, vets will be more than willing to lend support in the form of study material to help you to understand how you can take care of your cat at home.

Chapter 15: Feeding Your Himmie.

The centre of your cat's health is its diet. With the Himmie, it is very easy to plan its diet. They are not very fussy eaters. In fact, Himalayan Cats love to eat! They will enjoy just about anything that you feed them. As a result, it is very easy to go wrong with the diet of your Himalayan Cat if you do not pay attention to what you are feeding it.

Most Himalayan cat breeders and experts will recommend canned food instead of dry kibble. There are several long-term benefits in investing a little and providing your cat with nutrition rich foods. It is possible to avoid painful and life threatening illnesses by giving some thought to the kind of food that you give your Himmie.

Although some vets may recommend dry foods for Himalayan Cats, it is important to note that the health defects caused by kibble are many. It is also possible that the clinic and the curriculum of the veterinary clinic is funded by these pet food companies, making it mandatory for them to recommend dry kibble as a suitable option for your cat's diet. However, the truth is that the nutritional benefits of dry kibble are a lot lesser than the wet, canned foods.

a. Why no dry kibble?

Many cat owners prefer to give their cat dry kibble as it is more convenient in comparison to wet food. Of course the marketing strategies used and the alluring flavor choices make it harder for you to neglect them when you are out shopping for pet food. However, there are several health hazards associated with dry kibble that include:

- **Very low water content**

This puts your cat at the risk of extreme dehydration. If you look at dehydrated Himalayan Cat pictures , you will feel extremely unsettled and scared to give your cat any more dry kibble. There are other issues related to water deficiency including urinary tract diseases and malnutrition.

- **Too much carbohydrate:** This is a very common problem with regular intake of dry kibble. It leads to disorders like diabetes mellitus, obesity and also intestinal diseases. So if you think that dry kibble is good for a cat who is on a diet, think again. Even if you purchase low carb dry foods, the health issues associated with it are just as bad. These foods are water depleted and have very low nutritional value.

- **High in plant-based proteins** The cat's digestive system is designed for a carnivorous animal. They usually prefer eating meat and are, therefore, benefitted by animal proteins only. The intake of plant proteins is not really beneficial to the health of your cat as it only acts as a means to enhance the protein consumption in your cat.

Other health hazards of consuming dry foods:

- Bacterial contamination is common with dry foods. This may lead to severe vomiting and diarrhoea in the cat.

- Presence of fungal mycotoxins. They are usually found in grains and are extremely toxic for your cat.

- Insects. Sometimes insects and the feces of insects might be trapped in the packaged food. This can cause severe respiratory problems in your cat.

- Allergens that might cause severe allergic reactions in your cat may also be present.

Therefore, it is best that you provide your Himmie with canned foods along with other cooked meats.

b. Preventive Nutrition in Cats

Preventive nutrition is the best form of nutrition for your cat. If you think that your cat is "fine" and continue to give him foods that are not really recommended, there is a chance that he will develop serious health issues. For instance, cats who were constantly given dry foods suddenly developed the following conditions:

- Inflammatory Bowel Disease and asthma due to allergens

- Inflamed bladder leading to painful elimination of stools

- Blocked urinary tract that led to rupture of the bladder and death of the cat

- Feline Diabetes

- Kidney stones

Now, these conditions could have been prevented with a little attention to the food that the cats were given. As a pet owner, you must ensure that you choose a diet that ensures longevity and long-term health benefits for your cat. In order to understand preventive nutrition, here are some things that you must learn about the nutritional requirements in cats:

- The thirst drive is low in cats. Therefore, it is necessary for them to consume water along with their food. In the wild, the food that the cat eats will consist of almost 75% of water. Cats will never make up for the lack of water by sipping from their fancy water bowls.

- Water is extremely important to keep the urinary tract system healthy. If the necessary amount of water is not received by the cat's body, here may be harmful repercussion like urinary tract obstructions and also infections. These problems are not common in cats that normally consume canned foods or other forms of wet food.

- Carbohydrates are very damaging to your cat's health. They cause diabetes, which is one of the most common diseases in domesticated cats these days.

- Your cat is a carnivore by design. So feeding him plant-based proteins will only upset his digestive system.

- There are absolutely no benefits to the dental health of your cat from dry foods. Although several dry food companies may claim this, the fact is that there is no scientific basis to prove that this is true for cats.

Preventive nutrition is the only way to ensure that your cat has long lasting benefits from the food that it consumes. Of course, not all pet owners understand the principle that preventive nutrition is based upon.

With reference to the understanding what you have acquired from the points mentioned above, here are the four principles of preventive nutrition that you can follow to ensure optimized and holistic nutrition for your cat.:

Make sure that water is available with the food

Low carb foods, grain free foods and other 'healthy' versions of pet foods are not suitable for your Himmie. This is because they do not provide optimum nutrition for your cat. The digestive system of a cat is designed to acquire as much water from the food as possible. The food must contain between 65-70% of water. This is achieved only with canned foods.

It has been observed that dry foods are also cooked very harshly to provide the necessary texture and appearance. As a result, the nutritional value of these foods is greatly reduced. The amount of water consumed by a cat is the same whether you give it dry food or wet food. As a result, the total water consumed when the cat eats dry foods is reduced to almost half because there is no water present in the food itself.

Since the water consumed is substantially lower, the health hazards increase tremendously. Providing your Himmie with canned food is almost like flushing the digestive system. There are no risks of kidney and bladder related disorders if your Himmie consumes the recommended amount of water each day.

The diet should be high in animal proteins

There is a vast difference between animal and plant proteins. Unlike dogs that are omnivorous by nature, cats are strict carnivores. This means that your cat is an obligate carnivore. An obligate carnivore is an animal that has been designed to get all his nutritional requirements by consuming animal based proteins.

The proteins that are derived from animals are completely made of amino acids. This means that they have a complete amino acid profile. On the other hand, plant based proteins do not contain all the critical amino acids required by the carnivores. The amount of proteins available and the quality of proteins make up the biological value of the foods.

While humans and dogs can take the portions of amino acids available from plants to make the missing ones within the body, cats do not have this ability. So, a vegetarian diet or a diet rich in plant based proteins is never recommended for cats.

The quality of the protein is also quite poor in dried foods. This is because these foods are so harshly cooked that they lose their biological value. The reason that cat food makers use plant proteins is because they are cheaper than animal based proteins. This lets them make a higher profit margin. So they use sources like soy, rice and corn.

Avoid carbohydrates

There is no dietary requirement for carbohydrates in cats. Therefore, giving them too many proteins can actually be detrimental to their health. In dry foods, the average content of carbs is about 50%.

Carbohydrates alter the sugar balance in cats. As a result, the production of insulin is also altered. With canned foods, the amount of carbs present is between 3-5%. So, canned foods are a lot more beneficial to the cat's health. In its natural setting, a cat would never consume the amount of carbs that we feed it.

Provide Fresh Foods

Try to give your cat fresh, unprocessed foods. This will make it easy for them to derive the nutrients naturally and stay healthy.

These simple preventive nutrition measures will help you choose the right foods for your little pet. Remember that the more knowledge you acquire on cat health and nutrition, the better facilities you can give your cat.

c. Choosing the Right Cat Food

There is no doubt in the fact that cat food is extremely expensive. Of course, you must never compromise on providing your cat with the best options. There are some standards that can help you get maximum value for your money when you are out buying some chow for your cat.

Balanced with quality nutrients

Your cat requires water, energy and all the essential nutrients. The pet food that you buy must contain all these nutrients in the recommended quantity and must be easy to absorb. The actual source of the food is not directly influential on the health of your cat. It is the quality of the food that you provide for your cat that matters the most.

Just like humans, pets also require a diet that is well balanced. For cats, carbohydrates are not the right energy source. Instead, providing your cat with the right amount of protein will help him produce the required amount of energy. So, a diet rich in animal proteins, even if it does not have the required amount of carbohydrates, makes a good diet plan for your cat. No matter what form of pet food you buy, you must check the nutritional information. Usually, the good brands of pet foods will hire the most prominent nutritionists to formulate the contents of the cat food.

Food formulated by experts

Creating the right food for cats is not really easy. There is a certain amount of expertise that is very important to ensure that all the key ingredients and nutrients are present in the formulae. There are specialized pet nutritionists who strive to provide your cat with an optimized formula to ensure right nutrition. These foods are tested and tried for their effects before they are released for consumers to use. There are several feeding trials that are conducted to understand how effective the formula is in enhancing the health of your cat.

How many food trials have been conducted?

According to the Association American Feed Control Officials, feeding trials are the most important tools to understand the quality of the pet foods. The pet foods that have undergone feeding trials are given to the pets under recommended guidelines. The guidelines are followed strictly to make sure that the animals get the right nutrition from them. When you buy any form of cat food, look for this sentence: "AAFCO procedures substantiate that this food provides complete and balanced nutrition."

What are the Quality Controls that have been taken?

Safety is the primary concern when it comes to pet foods. There are several manufacturers who produce these foods in their own facilities. These companies are more trustworthy as a few important things are accomplished, such as:

– The quality control is better as the sources of the ingredients and all the associated processes can be monitored effectively.

– All the foods that are manufactured on site are held until they meet all the safety guidelines recommended for the product. As a result, issues like Salmonella contamination can be prevented effectively.

When you purchase a certain cat food, check if the food has been 'manufactured by' or just has been 'distributed by' the brand that you are choosing. If the brand that you are purchasing is also the manufacturing unit, it is easier to register complaints with respect to the quality of the food provided. You can report all the concerns that you have on the quality of the food to the manufacturer directly.

How Appropriate is it for your Cat?

There are several brands and types of cat foods available as per the activity level, age and breed of your cat. There are several "life stage foods" that have been formulated to suit the age of your cat. The nutritional requirements vary from kittens to adult and senior cats. However, there is another variety called the "ALL life stage" food. This is definitely not recommended as it may lead to malnutrition or even excessive nutrition, which could lead to several health issues in your cat.

If you find it hard to make a decision with the right food choice for your feline friend, you can simply take the help of store owners or salesmen who will know what is perfect for your cat. If you are still not convinced, the best person to talk to is your vet.

d. Foods you must never give your cat

The kind of food that your cat eats and you eat is extremely different. The entire digestive ability is quite different and hence, the food should also be significantly different. Many pet owners make the mistake of giving their cats the same food that is cooked in their home. Now, let's put it this way, do you think of dry kibble or canned fish as an appropriate food for you? Well, then how do you expect your cat to fulfill its nutritional requirements with the foods that you eat?

Usually pet owners think that their little beauties are sure of what is best for them. Cats are known to be picky eaters but there is little evidence that suggests that a cat knows what is right for it and what is wrong. Perhaps in the wild, cats follow their instincts and get the right nutrition. However, with domesticated cats, the varieties of foods that are available to them will make them reach out for all the wrong goodies.

Not only are these foods nutritionally poor, they can also be quite dangerous for your Himmie. As we mentioned earlier, it is very easy to feed your Himmie the wrong things. They will enjoy just about anything that you feed them. And, in the assumption that your cat is happy, you will continue to give him foods that can have serious health related issues. Here are 15 foods that are a complete no-no for your beloved Himmie:

Tuna

Although this does sound strange, there is a good chance that your cat will get addicted to tuna. Of course, a share of tuna now and then should not harm your cat too much. However, a steady tuna diet can cause malnutrition in your Himmie. Although cats savor tuna and really enjoy it, the nutrients available are not too many. Another common issue with tuna is mercury poisoning. Never keep open tuna cans within the reach of your cat. You can serve it occasionally but make sure that he knows that it is not available all the time.

Chives, Garlic, Onion

These are common ingredients in all our foods but they have disastrous health impacts on cats. Any form of these vegetables, cooked, powdered or even raw can cause anemia in cats by completely breaking down their red blood cells. Even though human baby food consists of powdered onion, do not consider it safe for your kitty. Onion poisoning and even gastrointestinal problems might arise if your cat eats chives, garlic or onion.

Dairy Products

Contrary to common belief, dairy products, including milk, are not advised for cats. They are able to tolerate and digest milk only when they are kittens. In adult cats, the digestive system is unable to process dairy products and therefore health issues like diarrhoea and other digestive issues become quite common.

Alcohol

Your cat must never, ever consume any form of alcohol. Make sure that all the liquor in your home is out of your cat’s reach. The effects on the cat's liver and brain are similar to the effects on the human brain. In cats, however, the amount of alcohol required to do this damage is a lot lesser. A 5 pound cat can go into coma with just two teaspoons of liquor. Even one teaspoon can be more can be fatal for your kitty. In pedigrees like the Himmie, the effect of alcohol is a lot worse.

Raisins and Grapes

Many cat owners consider grapes and raisins as suitable treats for their cats. This is never a good idea. Giving your cat too many raisins or grapes can also lead to kidney failure eventually. Even a small share of grapes can really make your cat fall sick. Vomiting is one early sign of illness caused by grapes. Some cats may have no reactions but we are not sure of the long-term effects of feeding grapes to your cat.

Caffeine

An overdose of caffeine can actually kill your cat. With caffeine intake, there is no antidote either. The most common symptoms of caffeine poisoning in cats include:

- Restlessness

- Fast Paced Breath

- Palpitations in the heart

- Muscle tremors

Caffeine is not only found in coffee. There are several other sources including beans, chocolates, colas and even energy drinks like red bull. Some medicines and painkillers also contain substantial amounts of caffeine.

Chocolate

It is impossible to say no to your adorable cat staring at you while you gorge on chocolate. However, this treat can end up being extremely harmful for your little pet. Chocolate consists of a toxic material known as theobromine. This is extremely dangerous for cats. It is found in all forms of chocolate including white chocolate. The common problems associated with chocolate are:

- Muscle tremors

- Seizures

- Abnormality in heart rhythm

- Death

Candy

Any sweetened food including candy, gum, toothpaste and baked goods contain an element called xylitol. This element can pace up the circulation of insulin in the cat's body. As a result, the level of sugar in the cat's body drops suddenly, causing seizures and liver failure in your Himmie.

Bones and Fat Trimmings

Scraps from the table are fed so often to cats. Fat and bone can cause serious health disorders in cats. Fat, whether cooked or uncooked, can result in vomiting, diarrhoea and intestinal problems in your cat. If a cat chokes on a bone, it can be fatal. Other problems related to the bones are lacerations and obstructions due to the splinters.

Raw Eggs

Many people believe that raw eggs are a healthy dietary option for their cat. However, this is not true. There are two primary health issues that result from the consumption of raw eggs. Firstly, food poisoning may occur due to the presence of bacteria like Ecoli. Secondly, a certain protein in the egg white, known as avidin, can reduce the absorption of vitamin B in cats, leading to skin related issues.

Raw Meat

Although many of you may argue that cats only eat raw meats in the wild, the truth is that uncooked meat and fish can be harmful to cats. They contain bacteria and microorganisms that might cause food poisoning. Additionally, certain enzymes present in raw fish can destroy essential vitamins like thiamine in the cat's body. This can cause neurological problems and can also result in a coma in extreme cases.

Dog Food

A bite once in a while will not harm your cat too much. However, the formula used in dog food is definitely not suitable for cats. Cat food is packed with necessary proteins and vitamins that can help the cat fulfill its nutritional requirements. On the other hand, dog foods can also contain plant proteins that are not suitable for your cat. If your cat regularly consumes dog food, it might become malnourished.

Liver

Giving your cat liver once in a while is not an issue. However, too much consumption of liver can lead to vitamin A toxicity in cats. This is a serious condition as it affects the bones. There might be deformities and also bone growths and spurts on the spine. Osteoporosis can also be observed in cats with vitamin A toxicity. In extreme cases it can be fatal.

Yeast Dough

Uncooked dough is never recommended for a cat. If it is consumed by the cat, there are chances that the dough will actually rise inside the cat's stomach. During this expansion, the dough may stretch the abdomen of the cat and also cause alcohol poisoning as the yeast ferments.

Often being cautious isn't good enough. Your cat might just make its way into your pantry and have a generous helping of restricted foods. There is no need to be alarmed. In most cases, your vet will be able to provide an antidote to take care of the situation for you.

e. Mistakes made while feeding a Himmie

We all love our cats. We definitely want the best for them. However, sometimes, we make silly mistakes that may jeopardize the wellbeing of our cats. The most common mistakes made are associated with feeding. Here are three mistakes that you must definitely avoid to ensure that your cat gets complete and wholesome nutrition:

Ignoring visits to the Vet

The best person to help your cat get optimum benefits from the food is the vet. Your vet can give you suggestions and recommendations about different cat foods that are available on the market. A vet is the best person to consult because they completely understand the condition of your cat's body. The recommendations made by the vet are based on scientific understanding.

In case there are any negative reactions of certain foods on your cat's body, your vet will be able to point them out. He can also recommend necessary nutrients to assist your cat's current health conditions. If your cat has been put under a therapeutic diet, your vet will be able to enhance the diet as required. So, you must never skip visits to the vet if you want to ensure optimum nutrition for your cat.

Ignoring the calories in the pet food

Whenever we buy processed foods for ourselves, we ensure that we check the nutrition chart on the packaging. We normally check for the calories and the fats that the particular food contains. The next time you buy some cat food off the rack for your beloved Himmie, make sure you do the same for his food.

Your cat must be put on a calorie conscious diet to make sure that he only receives the amount of calories he requires and nothing more. This precaution is necessary to make sure that your cat does not end up with unnecessary weight issues. Most pet foods that you can buy off the rack will have necessary details about the number of calories contained per serving.

These pet foods will also provide feeding guidelines that will tell you how you must provide your cat with a balanced diet. These guidelines are not always correct. If you are unsure of the serving size for your Himmie, the best person to talk to would be your vet. They will teach you how you can mix your cat's favorite treats with dry and mixed foods to keep his food interesting while maintaining a healthy weight.

Ignoring the amount of cat treats given to the cat

Many pet owners make the mistake of giving their cats too many treats out of affection. The truth is that several confectionaries that you choose as suitable cat treats consist of large amounts of toxins that can be fatal for your cat.

These treats may be favoured by your cats as they are very tasty. However, they are not of any nutritional value. Cats must be kept away from these treats, most importantly people food. You must allow a maximum of 10% of the cat's calorie intake to be from treats. Giving them too many treats can lead to lack of nutrition and eventual dehydration.

Taking these three basic precautions will help you give your cat the best nutrition possible. It might be hard to get over these feeding habits. You must put in a conscious effort, for the sake of your cat's health.

Chapter 16: Keeping Your Himmie Company

The Himmie may not be the ideal cat for your household. However, the immaculate beauty of the Himalayan Cat can make just about anyone fall in love with it. So, if you are unable to keep your Himmie company all the time, how do you make sure that he/she does not feel depressed or unhappy in your home?

a. Frequent travellers

Whether you are going on a vacation or even going out on a business trip, the biggest issue that you will face is making the right arrangements for your Himmie while you are away. You must ensure that your Himmie is in safe hands and is somewhere where he will be treated well and given a lot of love and affection. There are several options that are available, but the most common and reliable ones are:

Friends

If you are a cat lover, you must be in the company of several others who love and adore cats. There will definitely be someone in your group who can pitch in to take care of your cat while you are away. When you are handing this responsibility over to a friend, make sure that he or she has had pets in the past, preferably a cat. You must look for someone who will be able to make your cat comfortable and less anxious.

Family

If you have relatives who visit you regularly, leaving your cat in their care is a great idea. This is because your cat will be familiar with their smell and sight and will be able to adjust better in their company. If someone from your family is willing to stay over at your place and take care of your cat while you are away, it is the best possible deal.

Ask your Neighbor

If you have friendly neighbors who love cats, request them to take care of your Himmie. Neighbors, again, will be familiar with your cat and will therefore be able to comfort your cat while you are away. Not just that, the locality and the surroundings will not be too different for your cat to make adjustments to.

Find a pet sitter

There are several companies who will be willing to provide you with pet sitting services while you are away. Before you narrow down on one particular company, make sure that you are aware of the choices that you have before you. You can ask for recommendations from people who have availed these services in the past to choose the right company for your Himmie.

Meet the people at the company to understand their temperament and their ability to deal with cats. If you are sure that they are gentle, kind and, most importantly, responsible, you can do a trial run for one evening. If you see that they are good with your cat and that your cat is comfortable in their presence, you can give them the responsibility of taking care of your loved one while you are away.

Find a boarding home

There are several places where your cat will be boarded for the period that you are away. These professionals have all the necessary assistance. From people who feed and clean the cages to certified veterinarians, you will find that all the services are provided in these shelters. Of course, you can ask for recommendations before you actually decide to place your cat in a particular shelter. Make a visit to these places to check their standards of hygiene. The conditions of the cages, the staff available and the facilities available play an important role in the decision that you make.

If you have to travel, leaving your Himalayan Cat home alone, make sure that you take all the necessary measures to schedule your trip according to your cat. Plan well in advance and keep a list of options that are available to take care of your Himmie. Never rush these things at the last minute as you will end up making compromises on the necessary arrangements.

You can never say when an emergency will occur. In case you have to leave suddenly, you must be able to find the best assistance for your cat's care. So, it is a good idea to make a list of people who will always be willing to take care of your cat while you are away.

It is a good idea to make a chart of possible contacts and keep them near your phone so you can just reach out, pick up the phone and make sure your baby has a safe home to stay in.

b. Long working hours

If you are someone who works late hours, you might want to look for someone else to keep your cat company while you are away. If it is only occasionally that you get held up at work, you can just call someone from your caretakers' list to ensure that the cat is not alone. You must also make sure that there is someone to feed your cat on time when you are away.

If you frequently stay away from home, you can get yourself a pet monitor. These interesting devices will help you call out to your cat and also watch him all day long. Some modern devices also allow you to time a dispenser that will pop out treats as and when required. That way, your cat will never feel like he is at home all by himself.

You can definitely hire a full-time care taker for your cat. Make sure that you conduct a thorough interview before you actually appoint someone to take care of your cat. Inform this person about all the schedules of your cat. If your cat is under special medication or even a special diet, the caretaker must be informed well in advance.

The last option is to keep multiple pets at home. You can bring home another cat and allow your current pet and the new pet to get acquainted with each other. If you are just about to bring a pet into your home, a very good plan would be to just bring home two of them at once. They will grow up together and be able to keep each other company.

No matter what you do, the bottom line is that Himmies do not like to be left all alone at home. Even if it takes a great deal of effort from your end, make sure you keep your cat company whether you are gone for a couple of hours, or for days on end.

c. Travelling with your Himmie

Sadly, cats are not the best travel companions. If you have had a dog for a pet, never assume that your Himalayan cat will be as easy to travel with. With a Himalayan cat, it is mandatory to travel only in the colder months. They are very heat sensitive and will develop severe health problems if they are taken out in the sun. Whether you are travelling by car or train, make sure air conditioning is available to keep your Himmie comfortable.

Travelling in a car

Remember that you must never leave the cat to roam free in the car. If your cat decides to pounce on the driver, the repercussions could be fatal! Make sure that you always carry your cat in a carrier. The carrier should be extremely sturdy and must be made from metallic wires or even fiber glass. The carriers made from light plastic or even cardboard are not meant for long journeys. They are only suitable for short trips like a visit to the vet.

The weather that you travel in is extremely important in deciding what measures you need to take while travelling, if you think that it will get hotter as you proceed, make sure that you get a carrier that allows a good amount of air circulation. In case it is going to get cold along the way, carry enough blankets to wrap your cat up and keep him warm. There are also draft free carriers that will ensure that you do not leave your kitty shivering and uncomfortable. Irrespective of the kind of carrier that you buy, there is one more thing that you need to consider. In case you are planning to change your mode of transport along the way, plane for example, you must also check for the guidelines that they provide with respect to the type of carrier that is allowed.

If you have ample space in the back of your car and you only intend to travel by car, you can even use a large crate to keep your cat in. All you need to do is place blankets and sheets inside this crate and put it in the back of your car. The only thing that you need to ensure is that you provide your cat with a quiet place where he can rest during the journey. Place his favorite toys and treats around him to reduce the stress of travelling. The bedding that you provide during the travelling period should be the one that he is already used to.

Make sure that the crate or the carrier is completely secure. Even if you were to apply brakes suddenly, it must be safe. If the carrier or crate falls suddenly, your cat will be startled. The last thing you want while travelling is an anxious cat. If you are driving in a hatchback, never allow the cat to be placed in the boot as this area is very dark and badly ventilated. Check on your cat regularly and make sure that he is comfortable.

Travelling by train

When you are travelling by train, you must obviously place your cat in a carrier. Since there are several other strangers on a train, you do not want to have any instances of your cat breaking free and scaring them.

So, make sure that the carrier that you have is extremely sturdy. The base of the carrier must be extremely strong to ensure that your cat is secured. The carrier must be light so that you do not have any difficulty carrying it around. It must also be of a convenient size depending upon the space available on the train. Make sure that you get a carrier that is large enough for your cat to rest in. Never cram your kitty into a small carrier because there isn't enough storage space.

You must keep a familiar blanket in the carrier to reduce anxiety. However, littering and soiling can be quite a concern. So, line your cat's cage with a good amount of absorbent paper so that you may both have a pleasant journey.

Travelling by air

Travelling with your pet by air requires a good deal of planning in advance. The airlines that you choose will also vary with regards to their efficiency in handling and transferring your cat. Most airlines do not allow the transport of Himalayan cats as they tend to develop respiratory problems when they are in the plane. They may suffocate and die, even. So it is recommended that you avoid air travel. However, if you do find an airline that has the facility to transport a Himalayan cat, you must take several precautions.

Cats will have very little trouble travelling by air. If you have a pregnant cat or a kitten under three months of age travelling with you, it might become a matter of concern. It is recommended that you avoid air travel for these two categories of cats.

Check for a license to transport animals in the airlines that you choose. Chances are that you and your cat will travel by separate flights. If this is true, make sure that you get a direct flight for your cat so that it does not have to deal with issues like transits and transfers.

Travelling with your Himmie can be fun if you prepare your cat in advance. The most important thing to do is to condition it to enjoy sitting inside the carrier. If you are able to accomplish this, you have already won half the battle.

Chapter 17: Spaying or Neutering the Himmie

Breeding cats is a very time consuming procedure. In case you are unable to find the right mate for your cat when it is ready, chances are that it will develop a lot of aggression and behavioral changes. There are also chances of unexpected pregnancies when your Himmie mates with a stray. In order to avoid these difficult situations, it is best that you opt for spaying or neutering.

Spaying and neutering are special procedures carried out by prominent veterinarians to ensure that the cat is incapable of reproducing by removing the necessary organs. In the female cats, the fallopian tube, the uterus and the ovaries are removed while in the male, castration and removal of testicles is practiced. In females, this process is known as spaying, while in the males it is known as neutering.

a. Health Benefits of Spaying or Neutering

Spaying and neutering does not only curb the need to mate in your Himmie, it has several other benefits:

- Cats that have been spayed or neutered are less likely to develop breast cancer

- They will also not develop complications with the ovaries or uterus

- Neutered male cats are not at risk of testicular cancer

- Neutered male cats are also less likely to get into fights with stray cats

- These cats will not be infected by parasites and contagious diseases that affect stray cats and other cats.

The Importance of Spaying or Neutering

Feline overpopulation is a common problem these days. Even with a predominantly indoor cat like the Himmie, there are chances that the cat will mate with other strays. This may lead to kittens either in your home or on the streets. This is a problem either way as feline population has very painful and sad consequences. It is true that several shelters are euthanizing cats to make room for homeless kittens and also kittens that have been rescued.

If every cat owner takes the responsibility of neutering and spaying seriously, these unpleasant conditions can be controlled to a large extent.

Behavioral issues in cats that are not spayed or neutered

The most common problem with cats that have not been neutralized or spayed is the fact that they become very aggressive. Even though male cats are primarily territorial animals, they will engage in fights with other male cats. Female cats that are in heat also have a way of attracting stray male cats. They make a special yowling sound that calls out to all the male cats that are ready to mate.

b. Best time for spaying or neutering

Himmies must, ideally, be spayed when they are 6-9 months old. In most shelters, this is the age when the Himmie is neutered or spayed before they are sent out for adoption. To reduce the chances of aggression and also pregnancies, make sure you schedule to have your Himmie spayed or neutered before it begins to mark its territory. This is when you know that your cat is physically ready to find a mate. It you have a female cat at home, you must have her spayed to avoid any chance of pregnancy.

In case you have neglected spaying or neutering, you can even take your cat to the vet when he or she is in heat. However, with female cats, spaying when they are in heat will lead to excessive blood loss. If you think that you want your adult cat to be neutered or spayed, you can consult your vet about the safety of the procedure.

c. Behavior changes after neutering or spaying

There is no apparent change in the cat's personality after neutering or spaying. It is true that the cat might be quiet and calm and not too playful for a while but he or she will get back to its original self as soon as he/she recovers.

There are several myths that a Himalayan Cat will become lethargic or obese after neutering or spaying. This prevents most people from considering this rather important procedure. You may have to provide your cat with a certain diet after neutering or spaying. This is to ensure that the cat gets all the nutrients and calories required during the recovery process. If you have any concerns about the process of neutering or spaying, your vet will be able to provide you with all possible details.

d. Preparing the Cat

No matter what surgical procedure your cat is going to undergo, a good amount of preparation is mandatory. You can get all the necessary pre-surgical advice from your vet. Make sure you adhere to all the guidelines. The most common precaution to take is to ensure that your cat does not eat anything after midnight until the surgery. If you are taking a kitten for operation, on the other hand, the nutritional requirements are drastically different. Following these measures will ensure that there are no complications during the surgery and after:

The Recovery Process

Your cat might experience a little discomfort after the process. These procedures very seldom have a painful recovery process. If he is in pain, you must make sure you either leave him under specialized care or consult your vet regularly. There are a few precautions that you can take to ensure that the recovery process is comfortable and safe.

- Give your cat a safe place in the house to rest during the recovery process. This place should not be accessible by other pets or even children.

- Do not encourage jumping or running during this recovery process. You can take him out on walks but make sure that he is not physically exerted.

- The area that has been operated upon should not be licked. So, getting your cat an Elizabethan collar is the best option.

- During the recovery process, avoid using litter in the litter box. Instead, use shredded paper. The problem with sand or litter is that the dust can cause unwanted infections.

- The site with the incision must be cleaned regularly to avoid infections.

You must always look out for symptoms like:

- Redness at the site of incision

- Swelling at the site of incision

- Discharge from the area

- Reduced appetite

- Vomiting

- Lethargy

If you do notice one or more symptoms, inform your vet to improve the recovery process

Chapter 18: Breeding and Mating in Himalayan Cats

The Himalayan Cat reaches sexual maturity very early. A cat who is about 6-9 months old will be ready for a litter. Some Himmies may have a litter when they are just about 5 months old. But, before you proceed towards finding your cat a good mate, you must make sure that you understand the changes that take place in your cat's body and the actual mating process. Then, you might just realize that breeding is not the best option for your Himmie.

a. Reaching Puberty

When a male cat reaches puberty, he is known as a Tom. On the other hand, a female cat that hits puberty is known as the Queen. Puberty in male cats sets in when they are about 6-9 months old. Breeding a male cat is only a good idea if the litter that he came from was healthy and was of a good size. His mother should not have had any complications while giving birth. You can ask your breeder for this information before you buy your cat.

The female cat will experience multiple cycles of heat during the breeding season. This season usually starts in January or February and continues until October or November. The temperature during this season and the ratio between light and dark hours will play a significant role in your cat's heat cycle.

A female cat is ready to bear kittens at the age of 7 to 9 months. She will remain fertile for at least 9 years after she hits puberty. Only if your female cat comes from a healthy litter and a healthy mother should you consider breeding as an option. You can have your cat tested for the possibility of genetic disorders and illnesses to understand how safe or reasonable it is to choose the option of breeding.

Most female cats will show obvious signs before the actual heat sets in. You will see her roll around on the floor, rub herself against objects and also meow persistently. However, she will not allow a tom to mount her. This is not a sign of pain, as most owners presume. It is just your cat's hormones raging!

This heat cycle should last for about 8 days. The interval between one heat cycle and another is usually about 10 days. So expect your cat to exhibit this behavior at least twice in a month during the breeding season.

The hormonal changes that take place in the cat's body in this period are tremendous. While estrogen causes the onset of the heat cycle, progesterone takes over when she is pregnant. As the level of estrogen increases, the heat cycle will intensify. Once the level of estrogen drops, the heat cycle ends. This rise and fall of estrogen will only end when she is mated.

b. Finding the right mate

Cats are extremely sensitive creatures. Most often, they will be able to choose their own mates when you take them to the breeder. If your cat has not been neutered or spayed, make sure you take them to a good breeder, especially with a pedigree like the Himmie.

For Himalayan Cats, it is not necessary for you to pick another Himmie for mating. You can even outcross the cat with an American or British Short hair or a Burmese cat. Of course, if the goal is to achieve the same physical characteristics as the real Himmie, a pure parent breed is recommended.

You must always take a queen to the tom for breeding as she will not be too sensitive to these environmental changes during the mating process. The actual mating does not last for more than 4 minutes. Once this is over, the queen will break free by striking the male with her paw and turning away. The after reaction of the female is just cleaning herself after rolling and thrashing for a while. The after reaction may last up to 9 minutes.

If you are interested in producing a litter, you may have to allow your cat to be mated multiple times. With a single mating, there are only 50% chances of your cat getting pregnant. Studies show that female cats will allow up to 30 matings at intervals of 5 minutes.

One interesting fact about cats in general is that while each kitten has one father, the fathers of the kittens in a single litter may not have the same father. This is true because of the multiple mating process. As a result, your litter may have several varieties of kitten, depending upon the cats that your queen has mated with.

Chapter 19: Caring for a Pregnant Himmie

If your cat is pregnant, you will see the apparent abdomen size by the 16th day of pregnancy. If you are not experienced with cats, an ultrasound can help you decide if your cat is pregnant or not. There is an easy way to check if your cat is pregnant or not. If the uterus feels stringy, it means that your cat might be pregnant. By the 20th day of pregnancy, you can actually feel the kitten fetuses in the abdomen of the queen when she is relaxed.

Besides checking for pregnancy, ultrasound is also a useful tool to check if the development of the fetuses is normal. You can perform an ultrasound from the 26th day of pregnancy until the end of pregnancy. Enlargement and a pinkish tinge of the mammary glands will be observed as the pregnancy progresses. Pregnancy may last for about 69 days in your Himmie.

Important Tips and Guidelines

The pregnancy period is a very delicate one. You must ensure that you take the best care of your Himmie to have a healthy litter and also a safe delivery. Here are a few things to keep in mind while caring for a pregnant cat:

- Morning sickness is common in cats. Your vet will be able to provide you with assistance if this persists.

- Your pregnant cat may also reduce her food consumption by the third week of pregnancy.

- Overfeeding and weight gain during pregnancy can lead to complications during labor.

- The food that you give your queen must be highly nutritious.

- Protein and calcium are a must. However, never provide any supplements unless recommended by a vet.

- Your cat must be kept indoors during the last 15 days of pregnancy. This helps you ensure that she does not give birth elsewhere.

During your cat's pregnancy, you must make sure that you visit the vet regularly. The most important time for your veterinarian visit is during the last two weeks of pregnancy.

Is my Himmie in Labor?

There are some sure signs that will tell you if your beautiful Himalayan cat is ready to give birth. Here are some signs that you must look out for:

- Your cat will begin to nest

- Her body temperature will drop to about 99 F

- She will start lactating

- Her appetite will reduce

- She will show extreme behaviors. She will either become extremely affectionate or she will just become entirely reclusive.

Preparing for Birth

The one phase where you will experience maximum anxiety is when your Himmie actually gets ready to give birth. If you are not prepared, you will just end up fumbling and jeopardizing the health of your kitty. Here are some things that you must keep handy when your cat is in the last two weeks of her pregnancy:

- A sturdy cardboard box or a kittening box available at pet stores.

- Surgical gloves

- Syringe or an eyedropper to remove secretions from the nose and mouth.

- Cotton thread or Dental floss for the umbilical cord ties.

- Antiseptic for the umbilical stumps

- Scissors

- Clean and fresh towels

- The vet's number

- Milk replacer for kittens

- Emergency contact numbers

Now, all you need to do is prepare for the actual birth. When your cat is in the last week of her pregnancy, place the kittening box in a quiet spot. This spot should be warm and completely draft free. Place your cat's favorite blanket and some toys in this box to encourage her to sleep there.

The bedding that you choose for this kittening box should be comfortable for the kittens and shouldn't snag their claws. This bedding must be changed regularly after the birth of the kittens.

Danger signs

In case you observe one or more of the following symptoms, make sure you call your vet right away:

- Lack of appetite in your queen for 24 hours or more

- The temperature is high and continues to stay elevated

- She becomes lethargic

- She has unpleasant smelling discharge from her vagina

These are signs that something might have gone wrong during the delivery. They also indicate post natal stress in your cat and must be treated at the earliest.

Things you must not do during pregnancy

- Never use any flea powder or medicine without consulting your doctor first.

- Do not allow your Himmie to take any medication without a valid prescription

- Do not use antiseptics suitable for humans. These products, although mild on our skin may burn your cat's delicate skin.

- Avoid handling the kittens too much. Chances are that your cat will disown or even kill the kittens if they are threatened by intruders. Allow the kittens and the mother to bond.

- Do not allow your cat to roam around. Cats can get pregnant within 2 weeks of delivery. So keep her in confinement for a while.

- Do not de sex your cat until after 7 weeks of the kittens' birth.

Taking care of a pregnant cat is a huge responsibility. If you are not sure of how to go about it, you can look for a shelter or a veterinary hospital where the cats will be taken care of until the kittens are born. Once you have the kittens, you can decide if you want to keep them in your home or find them another loving home to live in.

Chapter 20: The Cost of owning a Himmie

Now that you are aware of the basics of cat care, you might begin to wonder how expensive it is to actually take care of one. In comparison to dogs, cats are cheaper to own. However, if you want to put a number on your cat care expenses, here is a clear break up:

The Cat

$900- $1200/ £500- 800

Depending upon the breeder and whether he/she gives you a pedigree certificate or not, this cost will vary. Sometimes, this cost may include necessary vaccines and also the de-sexing processes.

Council Registration

$40/ £25

Every cat that needs to be registered under the local council in some countries. This is necessary to obtain required licenses for your cat.

Desexing

$100-200 / £60-120

This is only if your breeder hasn't taken care of this already. The costs vary from one vet to another.

Microchipping

$50/ £30

In some countries, microchipping is mandatory. This is a good option to ensure that your cat, if lost, can be reunited with you at the earliest.

Vaccinations

$50-$70/ £20-£50

Never ignore or neglect vaccinations. In the first year, your cat will need about 3 vaccines.

Cat Carriers

$30-$50/ £15-£30

You will definitely need a cat carrier to make trips to the vet or travel with your beloved Himmie.

Scratching Post

$100 approx/ £60 approx

If you want to safeguard your home from havoc, make sure you get your kitty a scratch post. The costs may be higher depending upon the type of post you choose.

Cat Toys

$30/ £15 for basics

There are so many toys available on the market that you can certainly not put a price on this. However, for a basic selection, you will pay about $30. You must not neglect cat toys as they are necessary for good exercise for your cat.

Ongoing Costs

Food

$10/ £6 per week

There are various brands that you get on the market. The price of the cat food will depend entirely upon what you choose to feed your cat.

Litter

$8/ £10 per week

This is just an approximation. The costs may vary as per the type of litter.

Worming Medications

$2.50/ £1.50 per week

These topical medicines need to be re-applied regularly.

Veterinary checks

$70/ £40 per annum

This is the cost for routine checkups only. It does not account for unexpected accidents or illnesses.

Pet Sitter

$10- 25/ £5-10 per day

This is an expense that you cannot rule out if you are someone who travels occasionally or even works late.

Owning a pet is a big responsibility monetarily. It is as good as having a baby at home. If you think that you might have to compromise on any of the expenses mentioned above, make sure you re-think your decision of bringing home a Himalayan Cat.

Insurance

You might also consider taking out insurance for your cat. Usually, insurance policies are anything between $20 /£12 and $60 /£36 per month. Please be aware that the monthly cost for insurance might increase each year, as your cat gets older.

Chapter 21: Is the Himalayan Cat Right For you?

The Himmie is one of the most easy to accommodate cats. It will love you immensely and will get along very well with you and your family. If you already have other cats in your home, the Himmie is the best cat to include in your home as it is very compatible and friendly. When you are buying a Himmie, here are a few things that you must consider:

- How often do you travel?

- Does your job require you to work long hours?

- Is there a new born who requires a lot of your attention?

- Does your home have several strays visiting your yard often?

- Does your home provide enough place for your cat to hide and feel secure?

- Is your job too stressful?

The Himmie - Attention seeker

Although the Himmie is capable of adjusting to any type of household, the one thing you must keep in mind is that they require a lot of attention. If you are unable to give them the time that they require, the cat will definitely go into depression and be very unhappy.

Himalayan cats are not excessively vocal. However, when they feel neglected, they will talk to you. The voice of a Himmie is unusually shrill and when he is not getting the attention that he requires, his purrs will get louder and more resonant. So if you are someone who works really late at night and is already stressed at work, this quality might be extremely troublesome to you. This is also difficult if there are ailing people at home.

Not for Workaholics!

In case you are someone who brings his or her work home, there are very few chances that your Himmie will allow you to work in peace. Himmies love to stay by their owners side at all times. They will follow you around the house, rest on your lap and are all over you. So workaholics, beware! The Himmie is not the ideal cat for you.

Stay home with your Himmie

For people who travel very frequently, getting a Himmie is only inviting trouble. You can never leave your Himalayan Cat alone. They require constant interaction with people and also need that warmth all the time to feel comfortable and secure. If you still want to have a Himmie, you must make sure that you have at least one person who will come regularly to take care of your cat. Constantly changing your cat's caretaker will also make him extremely uncomfortable.

Ample Grooming Time

A Himalayan cat requires a lot of grooming. If you do not have the time or the patience to spend at least half an hour everyday fussing over your Himalayan beauty, you may want to reconsider your choice of cat.

Health issues

A Himalayan cat will require a lot of medical attention. They are prone to problems like breathing issues and also skin infections. You will have to invest a lot of time and money into making sure that your Himalayan cat is healthy. If your cat were to contract a disease like PKD, you must be willing to give it the care it needs.

So, there are several things that you must consider before you bring a Himalayan Cat home. This is one of the most beautiful breeds but if the Himalayan Cat personality does not suit you, you will regret this decision.

Chapter 22: The Best Things About a Himmie

The Himalayan Cat temperament is such that almost anyone will adore it from the word go! There are some specific traits of Himalayan Cats that make them the most preferred breeds across the globe. Whether it is a Pure Himmie or a Himmie Mix Breed, you will be able to find the following personality traits:

Extremely Affectionate

If you own a Himalayan Cat, you will need to look nowhere else for attention. Himmies are the kindest and the most friendly breeds that you will ever come across. Every single day, your Himmie will cry and wail when you are leaving home from work. He will wait until you get home. When you do get home, he will greet you like you have been gone for years. This affection is extremely fulfilling for the owners.

The Himmie will make the effort to talk to you about his day. He will follow you from one room to another until he finds a comfortable resting spot on you or around you. He will sleep next to you and let you cuddle his warm, fuzzy body. The best thing about the Himmie is his ability to get really attached and love unconditionally.

Very Adjusting

Whether you move into a new place, have new people living in your house or even include new pets into your household, your Himmie will only welcome the change. These cats take very little time to get along with new people and animals. When it comes to other pets in the house, the Himmie will, without a doubt, be extremely dominant. However, he will eventually make peace with any situation that he is put in.

Even when the Himmie is introduced to a new household, he will take no more than 2 days to come out of the Bonding Room to meet and greet the rest of your family.

Compatible with elders and children

Himalayan Cats are the most preferred breed for parents who have a new born in their family. Whether you have a toddler or an infant, be sure that your Himmie will be very gentle and patient. Even when children tease or play with a Himalayan Cat, they will seldom be scratched or bitten.

For seniors and elders, the Himalayan Cat is the most compatible partner as it will just laze around with them on the couch all day. A Himmie loves to stay indoors and be petted. This is the ideal condition for seniors who own cats. They will just make themselves comfortable on their lap and relax all day.

Chapter 23: Mistakes Made by New Himmie Owners

If you have just got yourself a Himalayan Cat, you must make its maintenance and safety your priority. When you bring home a new cat, you get so caught up in playing and petting your new beauty that you just brought home. However, there are several mistakes that new cat owners make. If you take cat care too lightly, there is a chance that your cat will not be happy and satisfied in your home. Here are a few pointers that will help you give your cat the best:

Underestimating the cost of owning a cat

Of course, bringing home a cat is not as expensive as bringing home a dog. This however does not mean that it is easy to have a cat at home. The expenses of taking care of the cat, its health and also the facilities that it requires can be quite a bit.

In addition to that, cats are a big responsibility. Now you will have to think twice before you plan a vacation. You will have to plan your entire schedule around your cat. If you are unable or unwilling to do that, owning a cat can be a serious problem for you.

Ignoring visits to the vet

You must make sure that you schedule regular visits to the veterinarian. If you neglect this, there is a good chance that you will not notice symptoms and signs of potentially hazardous diseases. Going to the vet will also help you understand if your routine with your cat is correct or not. In case you need to make changes in the diet or the amount of exercise that your cat gets, your vet can provide you with the assistance you require.

Failure to Spay or Neuter

Breeding or mating is not the easiest thing to do with cats. If you have ignored spraying or neutering, you will find your home in a mess during the time that your cat is in heat. It is common for male Himmies to pick fights with other male cats when they are not taken for mating in the right season. Female cats, on the other hand, will keep the entire household on their feet with constant purring and yowling when she is in heat. Given that the Himalayan Cat purr is loud and shrill, you do not want to find yourself in this situation. The worst thing that can happen to you is a litter of kittens when you are not prepared for it. Being unable to care for a pregnant cat or the kittens can be very stressful for you and your cat.

Buying Cheap Cat Food

If you try to save a few hundred dollars on your cat food, remember that you will end up paying several hundred dollars in helping your cat recover from nutrition related issues. Remember that your cat food must be a good source of protein. If you are unable to do that, your cat will be malnourished and unhealthy. Cheaper varieties of cat food will only be able to provide your cat with plant based proteins. For an animal that is an obligate carnivore, the only good source of protein is animal protein. In addition to this, these cheap foods also contain high amounts of carbohydrates that can make your cat obese or diabetic. Make sure you only bring home high quality foods for your pet.

Never allow your cat to roam outside

By nature, a Himalayan Cat likes to stay indoors. If you let him loose outside, chances are that he will consume food that is poisonous or hazardous to his health. He/she may also be attacked by bigger animals and get infected. Domesticated cats are not aggressive or defensive enough to take care of themselves in the great outdoors. It is true that your cat will get a lot of exercise outside. However, unsupervised visits outside the house are not recommended.

Neglecting litter box hygiene

Cats are very fussy about hygiene. If you do not clean the litter box regularly, you will notice peculiar behavior patterns like littering in other places inside the house. Some cats will also not eat well if the litter box hygiene is not maintained appropriately. Always examine the litter box and ensure that the litter is replaced on a regular basis.

If you are conscious, you can avoid these obvious mistakes. If you have any uncertainty about your cat's care, you can either speak to someone who already has a pet cat or you can ask your vet to assist you when required.

Conclusion

I am glad that you have chosen to seek some help in the care and nurturing of your Himalayan cat. This is a cat that is nothing but high maintenance. Afterall, the Himalayan cat has won over 40 pet shows since 1981.

If you are a Himalayan cat owner, I have no doubt that you are a proud parent. I hope that this book has all the information that you require with respect to your Himalayan cat. However, there is a final checklist that I would like to provide you with to make sure you do not miss out on anything.

- Keep an eye on your pet- I do not mean to tell you to become an obsessive parent. However, you must be sensitive to the changes that your cat undergoes physically and mentally. Adapt your home accordingly so that your Himmie never feels threatened.

- Grooming time is mandatory for a cat like the Himalayan cat. If you ignore this important step to taking care of it, you will find his coat tangled up in messy knots. The fur will become matted and chances are that your cat will develop several skin allergies.

- Treat it like the centre of your universe: Yes, this is mandatory with a Himalayan Cat. They are not forgiving if they are ignored or neglected.

- Make time to play: If your work comes first, do not even try to tell your Himmie that. They do not understand how you could possibly be too busy to play with them. Involve yourself in their playtime or you will find incessant meowing demolishing any chance of peace and quiet.

- Feed him or her well: Your cat is domesticated. It does not know to hunt for prey. You must keep a schedule and make sure that someone is always around to feed your cat on time. Unlike humans who would eat just about anything at any time of the day, cats are highly disciplined creatures.

- Get all the necessary licenses to ensure that your pet does not end up in a shelter. The laws with respect to pet registrations are very rigid and you must make sure you talk to your breeder about this.

- Your cat's health is priority. No matter how tired or lazy you feel, make sure you take your pet to the vet at the scheduled time. Any negligence in the department can have serious, and really expensive repercussions.

I hope you savor every minute of being the owner of a Himalayan cat. With this gorgeous breed in your home, you will be the envy of your entire social circle. But above all, you have a companion who will love you as long as he or she lives.

Published by IMB Publishing 2014

CPSIA information can be obtained at www.ICGtesting.com
Printed in the USA
BVOW02s1013100915

417436BV00023B/292/P